W9-CRR-306

THE
LITURGY OF THE HOURS

THE DIVINE OFFICE

revised by decree of the Second Vatican Ecumenical
Council and published by authority of Pope Paul VI

THE

LITURGY OF THE HOURS

According to the Roman Rite

Approved by the Episcopal Conferences
of The Antilles, Bangladesh, Burma, Canada,
of the Pacific CEPAC (Fiji Islands, Rarotonga,
Samoa and Tokelau, Tonga), Ghana, India, New Zealand,
Pakistan, Papua New Guinea and The Solomons,
The Philippines, Rhodesia, South Africa, Sri Lanka,
Tanzania, Uganda, and the United States of America
for use in their dioceses
and Confirmed by the Apostolic See

II

LENTEN SEASON

•

EASTER SEASON

English Translation Prepared by the
International Commission on English in the Liturgy

CATHOLIC BOOK PUBLISHING CO.
NEW YORK
1976

Concordat Cum Originali:

✠ James P. Mahoney, D.D.
Vicar General, Archdiocese of New York

English translation of the Liturgy of the Hours: General Instruction, Antiphons, Invitatories, Responsories, Intercessions, Psalm 95, the Canticle of the Lamb, Psalm Prayers, Non-Biblical Readings, and Hagiographical Introductions; original texts of the Opening Prayers and Alternative Opening Prayers from the Roman Missal, and the Roman Calendar.

For hymns and poetry see acknowledgments on page 2362

(T-402)

1 2 3 4 5 6 7 8 9 10 11 12 13 14 15

CONTENTS

6   Contents

Contents

Contents

SACRED CONGREGATION
FOR DIVINE WORSHIP

Prot. no. 1000/71

DECREE

From ancient times the Church has had the custom of celebrating each day the liturgy of the hours. In this way the Church fulfills the Lord's precept to pray without ceasing, at once offering its praise to God the Father and interceding for the salvation of the world.

The Second Vatican Council showed the importance of the traditional discipline of the Church and desired to renew that discipline. It was, therefore, very concerned to bring about a suitable restoration of this liturgy of prayer so that priests and other members of the Church in today's circumstances might celebrate it better and more effectively (see Constitution on the Sacred Liturgy, *Sacrosanctum Concilium*, number 84).

Now that this work of restoration has been approved by Pope Paul VI in the apostolic constitution *Laudis canticum* of November 1, 1970, this Sacred Congregation for Divine Worship has published the Latin book for the celebration of the liturgy of the hours in accordance with the Roman Rite, and it declares that the present edition is the typical edition.

Anything to the contrary notwithstanding.

From the Office of the Sacred Congregation for Divine Worship, Easter Sunday, April 11, 1971.

Arturo Cardinal Tabera
Prefect

Annibale Bugnini
Secretary

9

TABLE OF LITURGICAL DAYS

from the General Norms for the Liturgical Year and the New General Roman Calendar, nos. 59-61

The order of precedence for liturgical days is governed solely by the following table.

I

1. Easter triduum of the Lord's passion and resurrection
2. Christmas, Epiphany, Ascension, and Pentecost, Sundays of Advent, Lent, and the season of Easter
   Ash Wednesday
   Weekdays of Holy Week, Monday to Thursday inclusive
   Days within the octave of Easter
3. Solemnities of the Lord, the Blessed Virgin Mary, and saints listed in the general calendar, All Souls' Day
4. Proper solemnities, namely:
a) Solemnity of the principal patron of the place, city, or state
b) Solemnity of the dedication and anniversary of the dedication of a particular church
c) Solemnity of the titular saint of a particular church
d) Solemnity of the titular saint, founder, or principal patron of an order or congregation

II

5. Feasts of the Lord in the general calendar
6. Sundays of the Christmas season and Sundays in ordinary time
7. Feasts of the Blessed Virgin Mary and of the saints in the general calendar
8. Proper feasts, namely:
a) Feast of the principal patron of the diocese

11

b) Feast of the anniversary of the dedication of the cathedral

c) Feast of the principal patron of the territory, province, country, or more extensive territory

d) Feast of the titular saint, founder, or principal patron of an order, congregation, or religious province, observing the directives in no. 4

e) Other feasts proper to an individual church

f) Other feasts listed in the calendar of the diocese, order, or congregation

9. Weekdays of Advent from December 17 to December 24 inclusive

     Days within the octave of Christmas

     Weekdays of Lent

III

10. Obligatory memorials in the general calendar

11. Proper obligatory memorials, namely:

a) Memorial of a secondary patron of the place, diocese, region or province, country, or more extensive territory; or of an order, congregation, or religious province

b) Obligatory memorials proper to an individual church

c) Obligatory memorials listed in the calendar of a diocese, order, or congregation

12. Optional memorials, as described in the instructions indicated for the Mass and office, may be observed even on the days in no. 9

In the same manner obligatory memorials may be celebrated as optional memorials if they happen to fall on the Lenten weekdays

 3. Weekdays of Advent up to December 16 inclusive

   'Weekdays of the Christmas season from January 2

    ' the Saturday after Epiphany

     ~kdays of the Easter season from Monday after the

octave of Easter until the Saturday before Pentecost inclusive

Weekdays in ordinary time

CELEBRATIONS ON THE SAME DAY

If several celebrations fall on the same day, the one that holds the higher rank according to the above table is observed. A solemnity, however, which is impeded by a liturgical day that takes precedence over it should be transferred to the closest day which is not a day listed in nos. 1-8 in the table of precedence, the rule of no. 5 remaining in effect. Other celebrations are omitted that year.

If on the same day vespers of the current office and first vespers of the following day are to be celebrated, the vespers of the day holding the higher rank in the table of liturgical days takes precedence; if both days are of the same rank, vespers of the current day takes precedence.

PRINCIPAL CELEBRATIONS OF THE LITURGICAL YEAR

Year	Ash Wednesday	Easter	Ascension	Pentecost
1974	27 February	14 April	23 May	2 June
1975	12 February	30 March	8 May	18 May
1976	3 March	18 April	27 May	6 June
1977	23 February	10 April	19 May	29 May
1978	8 February	26 March	4 May	14 May
1979	28 February	15 April	24 May	3 June
1980	20 February	6 April	15 May	25 May
1981	4 March	19 April	28 May	7 June
1982	24 February	11 April	20 May	30 May
1983	16 February	3 April	12 May	22 May
1984	7 March	22 April	31 May	10 June
1985	20 February	7 April	16 May	26 May
1986	12 February	30 March	8 May	18 May
1987	4 March	19 April	28 May	7 June
1988	17 February	3 April	12 May	22 May
1989	8 February	26 March	4 May	14 May
1990	28 February	15 April	24 May	3 June
1991	13 February	31 March	9 May	19 May
1992	4 March	19 April	28 May	7 June
1993	24 February	11 April	20 May	30 May
1994	16 February	3 April	12 May	22 May
1995	1 March	16 April	25 May	4 June
1996	21 February	7 April	16 May	26 May
1997	12 February	30 March	8 May	18 May
1998	25 February	12 April	21 May	31 May
1999	17 February	4 April	13 May	23 May

PRINCIPAL CELEBRATIONS OF THE LITURGICAL YEAR

| | Weeks in Ordinary Time | | | | |
| | before Lent | | after Easter Season | | |
Corpus Christi	Number of weeks	Ending	Beginning	Number of weeks	First Sunday of **Advent**
13 June	7	26 February	3 June	9	1 December
29 May	5	11 February	19 May	7	30 November
17 June	8	2 March	7 June	10	28 November
9 June	7	22 February	30 May	9	27 November
25 May	5	7 February	15 May	6	3 December
14 June	8	27 February	4 June	9	2 December
5 June	6	19 February	26 May	8	30 November
18 June	8	3 March	8 June	10	29 November
10 June	7	23 February	31 May	9	28 November
2 June	6	15 February	23 May	8	27 November
21 June	9	6 March	11 June	10	2 December
6 June	6	19 February	27 May	8	1 December
29 May	5	11 February	19 May	7	30 November
18 June	8	3 March	8 June	10	29 November
2 June	6	16 February	23 May	8	27 November
25 May	5	7 February	15 May	6	3 December
14 June	8	27 February	4 June	9	2 December
30 May	5	12 February	20 May	7	1 December
18 June	8	3 March	8 June	10	29 November
10 June	7	23 February	31 May	9	28 November
2 June	6	15 February	23 May	8	27 November
15 June	8	28 February	5 June	9	3 December
6 June	7	20 February	27 May	8	1 December
29 May	5	11 February	19 May	7	30 November
11 June	7	24 February	1 June	9	29 November
3 June	6	16 February	24 May	8	28 November

PRINCIPAL CELEBRATIONS OF THE LITURGICAL YEAR

GENERAL ROMAN CALENDAR

JANUARY

1. Octave of Christmas
   SOLEMNITY OF MARY, MOTHER OF GOD
   Solemnity
2. Basil the Great and Gregory Nazianzen,
   bishops and doctors — Memorial
3.
4.
5.
6. EPIPHANY — Solemnity
7. *Raymond of Penyafort, priest★*
8.
9.
10.
11.
12.
13. *Hilary, bishop and doctor*
14.
15.
16.
17. Anthony, abbot — Memorial
18.
19.
20. *Fabian, pope and martyr*
    Sebastian, martyr
21. Agnes, virgin and martyr — Memorial
22. *Vincent, deacon and martyr*
23.
24. Francis de Sales, bishop and doctor — Memorial
25. CONVERSION OF PAUL, APOSTLE — Feast
26. Timothy and Titus, bishops — Memorial
27. *Angela Merici, virgin*
28. Thomas Aquinas, priest and doctor — Memorial
29.
30.
31. John Bosco, priest — Memorial
Sunday after January 6: **BAPTISM OF THE LORD** — Feast

★When no rank is given, it is an optional memorial.

FEBRUARY

1.
2. **PRESENTATION OF THE LORD**   Feast
3. *Blase, bishop and martyr*
   Ansgar, bishop
4.
5. Agatha, virgin and martyr   Memorial
6. Paul Miki and companions, martyrs   Memorial
7.
8. *Jerome Emiliani*
9.
10. Scholastica, virgin   Memorial
11. *Our Lady of Lourdes*
12.
13.
14. Cyril, monk, and Methodius, bishop   Memorial
15.
16.
17. *Seven Founders of the Order of Servites*
18.
19.
20.
21. *Peter Damian, bishop and doctor*
22. **CHAIR OF PETER, APOSTLE**   Feast
23. Polycarp, bishop and martyr   Memorial
24.
25.
26.
27.
28.

MARCH

1.
2.
3.
4. *Casimir*
5.
6.
7. Perpetua and Felicity, martyrs   Memorial
8. *John of God, religious*
9. *Frances of Rome, religious*
10.
11.
12.
13.
14.
15.
16.
17. *Patrick, bishop*
18. *Cyril of Jerusalem, bishop and doctor*
19. JOSEPH, HUSBAND OF MARY   Solemnity
20.
21.
22.
23. *Turibius de Mongrovejo, bishop*
24.
25. ANNUNCIATION   Solemnity
26.
27.
28.
29.
30.
31.

APRIL

1.
2. *Francis of Paola, hermit*
3.
4. *Isidore, bishop and doctor*
5. *Vincent Ferrer, priest*
6.
7. John Baptist de la Salle, priest   Memorial
8.
9.
10.
11. *Stanislaus, bishop and martyr*
12.
13. *Martin I, pope and martyr*
14.
15.
16.
17.
18.
19.
20.
21. *Anselm, bishop and doctor*
22.
23. *George, martyr*
24. *Fidelis of Sigmaringen, priest and martyr*
25. MARK, EVANGELIST   Feast
26.
27.
28. *Peter Chanel, priest and martyr*
29. Catherine of Siena, virgin and doctor   Memorial
30. *Pius V, pope*

MAY

1. *Joseph the Worker*
2. **Athanasius, bishop and doctor**   Memorial
3. PHILIP AND JAMES, APOSTLES   Feast
4.
5.
6.
7.
8.
9.
10.
11.
12. *Nereus and Achilleus, martyrs*
    Pancras, martyr
13.
14. MATTHIAS, APOSTLE   Feast
15.
16.
17.
18. *John I, pope and martyr*
19.
20. *Bernardine of Siena, priest*
21.
22.
23.
24.
25. *Venerable Bede, priest and doctor*
    Gregory VII, pope
    Mary Magdalene de Pazzi, virgin
26. **Philip Neri, priest**   Memorial
27. *Augustine of Canterbury, bishop*
28.
29.
30.
31. VISITATION   Feast

First Sunday after Pentecost: **HOLY TRINITY**   Solemnity
Thursday after Holy Trinity: **CORPUS CHRISTI** Solemnity
Friday following Second Sunday after Pentecost:
    SACRED HEART   Solemnity
Saturday following Second Sunday after Pentecost:
    Immaculate Heart of Mary

JUNE

1. Justin, martyr　　　　　　　　　　　　　　　Memorial
2. *Marcellinus and Peter, martyrs*
3. Charles Lwanga and companions, martyrs　　　Memorial
4.
5. Boniface, bishop and martyr　　　　　　　　Memorial
6. *Norbert, bishop*
7.
8.
9. *Ephrem, deacon and doctor*
10.
11. Barnabas, apostle　　　　　　　　　　　　　Memorial
12.
13. Anthony of Padua, priest and doctor　　　　Memorial
14.
15.
16.
17.
18.
19. *Romuald, abbot*
20.
21. Aloysius Gonzaga, religious　　　　　　　　Memorial
22. *Paulinus of Nola, bishop*
    John Fisher, bishop and martyr, and
    　　Thomas More, martyr
23.
24. BIRTH OF JOHN THE BAPTIST　　　　　Solemnity
25.
26.
27. *Cyril of Alexandria, bishop and doctor*
28. Irenaeus, bishop and martyr　　　　　　　　Memorial
29. PETER AND PAUL, APOSTLES　　　　　Solemnity
30. *First Martyrs of the Church of Rome*

JULY

1.
2.
3. THOMAS, APOSTLE   Feast
4. *Elizabeth of Portugal*
5. *Anthony Zaccaria, priest*
6. *Maria Goretti, virgin and martyr*
7.
8.
9.
10.
11. Benedict, abbot   Memorial
12.
13. *Henry*
14. *Camillus de Lellis, priest*
15. Bonaventure, bishop and doctor   Memorial
16. *Our Lady of Mount Carmel*
17.
18.
19.
20.
21. *Lawrence of Brindisi, priest and doctor*
22. Mary Magdalene   Memorial
23. *Bridget, religious*
24.
25. JAMES, APOSTLE   Feast
26. Joachim and Ann, parents of Mary   Memorial
27.
28.
29. Martha   Memorial
30. *Peter Chrysologus, bishop and doctor*
31. Ignatius of Loyola, priest   Memorial

AUGUST

1. Alphonsus Liguori, bishop and doctor — Memorial
2. *Eusebius of Vercelli, bishop*
3.
4. John Vianney, priest — Memorial
5. *Dedication of St. Mary Major*
6. TRANSFIGURATION — Feast
7. *Sixtus II, pope and martyr, and companions, martyrs*
   Cajetan, priest
8. Dominic, priest — Memorial
9.
10. LAWRENCE, DEACON AND MARTYR — Feast
11. Clare, virgin — Memorial
12.
13. *Pontian, pope and martyr, and Hippolytus,*
    priest and martyr
14.
15. ASSUMPTION — Solemnity
16. *Stephen of Hungary*
17.
18.
19. *John Eudes, priest*
20. Bernard, abbot and doctor — Memorial
21. Pius X, pope — Memorial
22. Queenship of Mary — Memorial
23. *Rose of Lima, virgin*
24. BARTHOLOMEW, APOSTLE — Feast
25. *Louis*
    Joseph Calasanz, priest
26.
27. Monica — Memorial
28. Augustine, bishop and doctor — Memorial
29. Beheading of John the Baptist, martyr — Memorial
30.
31.

SEPTEMBER

1.
2.
3. Gregory the Great, pope and doctor　　　　Memorial
4.
5.
6.
7.
8. BIRTH OF MARY　　　　Feast
9.
10.
11.
12.
13. John Chrysostom, bishop and doctor　　　Memorial
14. TRIUMPH OF THE CROSS　　　　Feast
15. Our Lady of Sorrows　　　　Memorial
16. Cornelius, pope and martyr, and
　　　Cyprian, bishop and martyr　　　　Memorial
17. *Robert Bellarmine, bishop and doctor*
18.
19. *Januarius, bishop and martyr*
20.
21. MATTHEW, APOSTLE AND EVANGELIST　　Feast
22.
23.
24.
25.
26. *Cosmas and Damian, martyrs*
27. Vincent de Paul, priest　　　　Memorial
28. *Wenceslaus, martyr*
29. MICHAEL, GABRIEL, AND RAPHAEL,
　　　ARCHANGELS　　　　Feast
30. Jerome, priest and doctor　　　　Memorial

OCTOBER

1. Theresa of the Child Jesus, virgin   Memorial
2. Guardian Angels   Memorial
3.
4. Francis of Assisi   Memorial
5.
6. *Bruno, priest*
7. Our Lady of the Rosary   Memorial
8.
9. *Denis, bishop and martyr, and companions, martyrs*
   John Leonardi, priest
10.
11.
12.
13.
14. *Callistus I, pope and martyr*
15. Teresa of Avila, virgin and doctor   Memorial
16. *Hedwig, religious*
    Margaret Mary Alacoque, virgin
17. Ignatius of Antioch, bishop and martyr   Memorial
18. LUKE, EVANGELIST   Feast
19. *Isaac Jogues and John de Brebeuf, priests and*
    martyrs, and companions, martyrs
    Paul of the Cross, priest
20.
21.
22.
23. *John of Capistrano, priest*
24. *Anthony Claret, bishop*
25.
26.
27.
28. SIMON AND JUDE, APOSTLES   Feast
29.
30.
31.

NOVEMBER

1. ALL SAINTS   Solemnity
2. ALL SOULS
3. *Martin de Porres, religious*
4. Charles Borromeo, bishop   Memorial
5.
6.
7.
8.
9. DEDICATION OF ST. JOHN LATERAN   Feast
10. Leo the Great, pope and doctor   Memorial
11. Martin of Tours, bishop   Memorial
12. Josaphat, bishop and martyr   Memorial
13.
14.
15. *Albert the Great, bishop and doctor*
16. *Margaret of Scotland*
    Gertrude, virgin
17. Elizabeth of Hungary, religious   Memorial
18. *Dedication of the churches of Peter and Paul, apostles*
19.
20.
21. Presentation of Mary   Memorial
22. Cecilia, virgin and martyr   Memorial
23. *Clement I, pope and martyr*
    Columban, abbot
24.
25.
26.
27.
28.
29.
30. ANDREW, APOSTLE   Feast

Last Sunday in Ordinary Time:
    CHRIST THE KING   Solemnity

DECEMBER

1.
2.
3. Francis Xavier, priest   Memorial
4. *John Damascene, priest and doctor*
5.
6. *Nicholas, bishop*
7. Ambrose, bishop and doctor   Memorial
8. IMMACULATE CONCEPTION   Solemnity
9.
10.
11. *Damasus I, pope*
12. *Jane Frances de Chantal, religious*
13. Lucy, virgin and martyr   Memorial
14. John of the Cross, priest and doctor   Memorial
15.
16.
17.
18.
19.
20.
21. *Peter Canisius, priest and doctor*
22.
23. *John of Kanty, priest*
24.
25. CHRISTMAS   Solemnity
26. STEPHEN, FIRST MARTYR   Feast
27. JOHN, APOSTLE AND EVANGELIST   Feast
28. HOLY INNOCENTS, MARTYRS   Feast
29. *Thomas Becket, bishop and martyr*
30.
31. *Sylvester I, pope*

Sunday within the octave of Christmas or if there is
no Sunday within the octave, December 30:
HOLY FAMILY   Feast

PROPER CALENDAR FOR THE DIOCESES OF THE UNITED STATES OF AMERICA

JANUARY

4. Elizabeth Ann Seton   Memorial
5. Blessed John Neumann, bishop   Memorial

MAY

15. *Isidore*

JULY

4. *Independence Day*

SEPTEMBER

9. Peter Claver, priest   Memorial

OCTOBER

19. Isaac Jogues and John de Brebeuf, priests
    and martyrs, and companions, martyrs   Memorial

NOVEMBER

13. Frances Xavier Cabrini, virgin   Memorial
Fourth Thursday *Thanksgiving Day*

DECEMBER

12. Our Lady of Guadalupe   Memorial

PROPER OF SEASONS

LENTEN SEASON

I. Before Holy Week

The following hymns may be sung during the Lenten Season until Holy Week.

Evening Prayer

HYMN

Lord, who throughout these forty days
For us did fast and pray,
Teach us with you to mourn our sins,
And close by you to stay.

As you with Satan did contend
And did the vict'ry win,
O give us strength in you to fight,
In you to conquer sin.

As you did hunger and did thirst,
So teach us, gracious Lord,
To die to self and so to live
By your most holy word.

Abide with us, that through this life
Of suff'ring and of pain
An Easter of unending joy
We may at last attain.

Melody: St. Flavian C.M.   Music: Day's *Psalter*, 1562
                     Text: Claudia Hernaman, 1838-1898, alt.

Or:

This is our accepted time,
This is our salvation;
Prayer and fasting are our hope,
Penance, our vocation.

33

God of pardon and of love,
Mercy past all measure,
You alone can grant us peace,
You, our holy treasure.

Lord, look down upon your sons,
Look upon their yearning;
Man is dust, and unto dust
He shall be returning.
Lift him up, O Lord of life,
Flesh has gained him sadness,
Hear his plea, bestow on him
Everlasting gladness.

Melody: Weimar 76.76.D   Music: Melchior Vulpius, 1609
                                Text: Michael Gannon, alt., 1955

Or:

Refrain:

Draw near, O Lord, our God, graciously hear us,
Guilty of sinning before you.

O King exalted, Savior of all nations,
See how our grieving lifts our eyes to heaven;
Hear us, Redeemer, as we beg forgiveness.

Refrain

Might of the Father, Keystone of God's temple,
Way of salvation, Gate to heaven's glory;
Sin has enslaved us; free your sons from bondage.

Refrain

We pray you, O God, throned in strength and
    splendor,
ear from your kingdom this, our song of sorrow:
    w us your mercy, pardon our offenses.

Refrain

Humbly confessing countless sins committed,
Our hearts are broken, laying bare their secrets;
Cleanse us, Redeemer, boundless in compassion.

Refrain

Innocent captive, unresisting victim,
Liars denounced you, sentenced for the guilty;
Once you redeemed us: now renew us, Jesus.

Refrain

Melody: Draw Near, O Lord   Music: Paris Processional, 1824
Text: Attende, Domine
Translator: Melvin Farrell, S.S., 1961

Or:

When I survey the wondrous cross
On which the Prince of glory died,
My richest gain I count but loss,
And pour contempt on all my pride.

Forbid it, Lord, that I should boast,
Save in the death of Christ my God;
The vain delights that charm me most:
I sacrifice them to his blood.

See from his head, his hands, his feet
What grief and love flow mingling down;
Did e'er such Love and sorrow meet,
Or thorns compose so rich a crown?

Were all the realm of nature mine,
That were a present far too small;
Love so amazing, so divine,
Demands my soul, my life, my all.

Melody: Rockingham L.M.   Music: Adapted by Edward Miller,
1731-1807, from A. William's *A Second
Supplement to Psalmody in Miniature*,
Oxford, c. 1780
Text: Isaac Watts, 1674-1748, slightly adapted

Or:

Antiphon:
Keep in mind that Jesus Christ has died for us
and is risen from the dead.
He is our saving Lord,
he is joy for all ages.

If we die with the Lord,
we shall live with the Lord.

Antiphon

If we endure with the Lord,
we shall reign with the Lord.

Antiphon

In him all our sorrow,
in him all our joy.

Antiphon

In him hope of glory,
in him all our love.

Antiphon

In him our redemption,
in him all our grace.

Antiphon

In him our salvation,
in him all our peace.

Antiphon

Melody: Keep in Mind

Music: Lucien Deiss, 1965
Text: Lucien Deiss, 1965

Or:

Audi, benigne Conditor,
nostras preces cum fletibus,

sacrata in abstinentia
fusas quadragenaria.

Scrutator alme cordium,
infirma tu scis virium;
ad te reversis exhibe
remissionis gratiam.

Multum quidem peccavimus,
sed parce confitentibus,
tuique laude nominis
confer medelam languidis.

Sic corpus extra conteri
dona per abstinentiam,
ieiunet ut mens sobria
a labe prorsus criminum.

Praesta, beata Trinitas,
concede, simplex Unitas,
ut fructuosa sint tuis
haec parcitatis munera. Amen.

Or:

Iesu, quadragenariae,
dicator abstinentiae,
qui ob salutem mentium
praeceperas ieiunium,

Adesto nunc Ecclesiae,
adesto paenitentiae,
qua supplicamur cernui
peccata nostra dilui.

Tu retroacta crimina
tua remitte gratia
et a futuris adhibe
custodiam mitissime,

Ut, expiati annuis
compunctionis actibus,
tendamus ad paschalia
digne colenda gaudia.

Te rerum universitas,
clemens, adoret, Trinitas,
et nos novi per veniam
novum canamus canticum. Amen.

Night Prayer

HYMN

The Master came to bring good news,
The news of love and freedom,
To heal the sick and seek the poor,
To build the peaceful kingdom.

Refrain:

Father, forgive us! Through Jesus, hear us!
As we forgive one another.

Through Jesus Christ the Law's fulfilled,
The man who lived for others.
The law of Christ is love alone,
To serve now all our brothers.

Refrain

To seek the sinners Jesus came,
To live among the friendless,
To show them love that they might share
The kingdom that is endless.

Refrain

Forgive us, Lord, as we forgive
And seek to help each other.

Forgive us, Lord, and we shall live
To pray and work together.

Refrain

Melody: Ich Glaub An Gott 87.87   Music: Mainz *Gesangbuch*,
with Refrain   1833
                                    Text: Gabriel Huck, 1965

Or:

When from the darkness comes no light,
When from the weeping comes no laughter;
When in the day we hope for night
Nor any comfort coming after:
Grant us your peace

When in our confidence our fears
Clutch at the heart and make us tremble;
When in our joy we weep cold tears,
And in our frankness we dissemble:
Grant us your light.

When in our love there is not care,
And in our yearning we are dullness;
When what we know we cannot dare,
And we are nothing that is fullness:
Grant us your truth.

Melody: Courtney 89.89.4   Music: Colin Mawby, 1971
                             Text: Brendan McLaughlin, 1971

Or:

Let all mortal flesh keep silence,
And with fear and trembling stand;
Ponder nothing earthly-minded,
For with blessing in his hand
Christ our Lord to earth descends now,
Our full homage to demand.

Rank on rank the host of heaven
Spreads its vanguard on the way,
As the Light of Light descends now
From the realms of endless day,
That the powers of hell may vanish
As the darkness clears away.

Melody: Picardy 87.87.87   Music: Melody from *Chansons Populaires des Provinces de France,* 1860
Text: *Liturgy of Saint James,* paraphrased by Gerard Moultrie, 1864, alt.

Invitatory

On Sundays and weekdays:

Ant.   Come, let us worship Christ the Lord, who for our sake endured temptation and suffering.

Or: Today if you hear the voice of the Lord, harden not your hearts.

Invitatory psalm, as in the Ordinary, 1044.

Office of Readings

HYMN

Now let us all with one accord
In fellowship with ages past,
Keep vigil with our heav'nly Lord,
In his temptation and his fast.

The covenant, so long revealed
To faithful men in former time,
Christ by his own example sealed,
The Lord of love, in love sublime.

This love, O Lord, we sinful men
Have not returned, but falsified;

Author of mercy, turn again
And see our sorrow for our pride.

Remember, Lord, though frail we be,
By your own kind hand were we made;
And help us, lest our frailty
Cause your great name to be betrayed.

Therefore we pray you, Lord, forgive;
So when our wanderings here shall cease,
We may with you for ever live,
In love and unity and peace.

Hear us, O Trinity sublime,
And undivided unity;
So let this consecrated time
Bring forth its fruit abundantly.

Melody: Schütz' Psalm 66 L.M. Music: Heinrich Schütz,
1585-1672, alt.
Text: Ex more docti, attributed to
Saint Gregory the Great
Translator: Editors of *Praise the Lord*, 1972

Or:

Creator of the earth and skies,
To whom all truth and power belong,
Grant us your truth to make us wise;
Grant us your power to make us strong.

We have not known you: to the skies
Our monuments of folly soar,
And all our self-wrought miseries
Have made us trust ourselves the more.

We have not loved you: far and wide
The wreckage of our hatred spreads,
And evils wrought by human pride
Recoil on unrepentant heads.

We long to end this worldwide strife:
How shall we follow in your way?
Speak to mankind your words of life,
Until our darkness turns to day.

Melody: Uffingham or
Creator Alme Siderum L.M.

Music: (Uffingham) J. Clarke,
c. 1659-1707, or (Creator
Alme Siderum) Gregorian
Text: Donald Hughes, 1911-1967, alt.

Or:

Antiphon:

Lord, your glory in Christ we have seen,
Full of goodness and full of grace:
In Christ let us live anew,
Fill us with his love,
And all men shall see the Fruits of your victory.

The Almighty has planted his Seed in the earth:
He tended well the grain, and he waits for rebirth.

Antiphon

The Almighty has ground all the grain for the feast:
He made it into flour, and he waits for the yeast.

Antiphon

The Almighty has given his body for man:
He broke for us the bread, and he waits like a lamb.

Antiphon

The Almighty was given a crown made of thorn:
It pierced him till he bled, and he waits: do we
mourn?

Antiphon

The Almighty did suffer and evil destroy:
He died to ease our pain, and he waits for our joy.

Antiphon

Melody: Dieu, Nous   Music: Jean Langlais
Avons Vu Ta Gloire   Text: *Dieu, Nous Avons Vu Ta
                                      Gloire,* Didier Rimaud
                                Translator: Anthony G. Petti

Morning Prayer

HYMN

Praise to the holiest in the height,
And in the depth be praise,
In all his words most wonderful,
Most sure in all his ways.

O loving wisdom of our God!
When all was sin and shame,
A second Adam to the fight
And to the rescue came.

O wisest love! that flesh and blood
Which did in Adam fail,
Should strive afresh against their foe,
Should strive and should prevail;

And that a higher gift than grace
Should flesh and blood refine,
God's presence and his very self
And essence all divine.

O generous love! that he who smote
In man for man the foe,
The double agony in man
For man should undergo;

And in the garden secretly,
And on the cross on high,
Should teach his brethren, and inspire
To suffer and to die.

Praise to the holiest in the height,
And in the depth be praise,
In all his words most wonderful,
Most sure in all his ways.

Melody: Billing C.M.   Music: Richard R. Terry, 1865-1938
Text: J. H. Newman, 1801-1890

Or:

The glory of these forty days
We celebrate with songs of praise;
For Christ, by whom all things were made,
Himself has fasted and has prayed.

Alone and fasting Moses saw
The loving God who gave the law;
And to Elijah, fasting, came
The steeds and chariots of flame.

So Daniel trained his mystic sight,
Deliver'd from the lions' might;
And John, the Bridegroom's friend, became
The herald of Messiah's name.

Then grant us, Lord, like them to do
Such things as bring great praise to you;
Our spirits strengthen with your grace
And give us joy to see your face.

O Father, Son, and Spirit blest,
To you be every prayer addressed
And by all mankind be adored,
From age to age, the only Lord.

Melody: Erhalt' uns, Herr   Music: J. Klug's *Geistliche Lieder*,
1547

Text: Latin, 6th century
Translator: Maurice F. Bell, 1906, alt.

Or:

Antiphon:

Grant to us, O Lord, a heart renewed;
Recreate in us your own Spirit, Lord!

Behold, the days are coming, says the Lord our God,
When I will make a new convenant with the house
of Israel.

Antiphon

Deep within their being I will implant my law,
I will write it in their hearts.

Antiphon

I will be their God, and they shall be my people.

Antiphon

And for all their faults I will grant forgiveness;
Never more will I remember their sins.

Antiphon

Melody: Grant To Us   Music: Lucien Deiss, C.S.Sp., 1965
                             Text: Lucien Deiss, C.S.Sp., 1965

Or:

With hearts renewed by living faith,
We lift our thoughts in grateful prayer
To God our gracious Father,
Whose plan it was to make us sons
Through his own Son's redemptive death,
That rescued us from darkness.
Lord, God, Savior,
Give us strength to mold our hearts in your true
likeness.
Sons and servants of our Father.

So rich God's grace in Jesus Christ,
That we are called as sons of light
To bear the pledge of glory.
Through him in whom all fullness dwells,
We offer God our gift of self
In union with the Spirit.
Lord, God, Savior,
Give us strength to mold our hearts in your true
    likeness.
Sons and servants of our Father.

Melody: Frankfort 887.887.48.48   Music: Philip Nicolai, 1599,
                                          arr. by J. S. Bach, c. 1730
                                          Text: Jack May, S.J.

Or:

Precemur omnes cernui,
clamemus atque singuli,
ploremus ante iudicem,
flectamus iram vindicem:

Nostris malis offendimus
tuam, Deus, clementiam;
effunde nobis desuper,
remissor, indulgentiam.

Memento quod sumus tui,
licet caduci, plasmatis;
ne des honorem nominis
tui, precamur, alteri.

Laxa malum quod fecimus,
auge bonum quod poscimus,
placere quo tandem tibi
possimus hic et perpetim.

Praesta, beata Trinitas,
concede, simplex Unitas,

ut fructuosa sint tuis
haec parcitatis munera. Amen.

Or:

Iam, Christe, sol iustitiae,
mentis dehiscant tenebrae,
virtutum ut lux redeat,
terris diem cum reparas.

Dans tempus acceptabile
et paenitens cor tribue,
convertat ut benignitas
quos longa suffert pietas;

Quiddamque paenitentiae
da ferre, quo fit demptio,
maiore tuo munere,
culparum quamvis grandium.

Dies venit, dies tua,
per quam reflorent omnia;
laetemur in hac ut tuae
per hanc reducti gratiae.

Te rerum universitas,
clemens, adoret, Trinitas,
et nos novi per veniam
novum canamus canticum. Amen.

Daytime Prayer

HYMN

Take up your cross, the Savior said,
If you would my disciple be;
Deny yourself, the world forsake,
And humbly follow after me.

Take up your cross, let not its weight
Fill your weak spirit with alarm;
His strength shall bear your spirit up,
Shall brace your heart and nerve your arm.

Take up your cross then in his strength,
And ev'ry danger calmly brave,
To guide you to a better home,
And vict'ry over death and grave.

Take up your cross and follow Christ,
Nor think till death to lay it down;
For only he who bears the cross
May hope to wear the glorious crown.

To you, great Lord, the One in three,
All praise for evermore ascend;
O grant us here below to see
The heav'nly life that knows no end.

Melody: Breslau or
Winchester New L.M.

Music: (Breslau) *As Hymnodus sacer,*
1625, or (Winchester New) *Musika-*
lisches Handbuch, Hamburg, 1690
Text: Charles William Everest, 1814-1877,
adapted by Anthony G. Petti

ASH WEDNESDAY

Psalter, Week IV

Office of Reading

HYMN, 40.
Psalms from Wednesday, Week IV, 155.

Turn back to the Lord and do penance.
—Be renewed in heart and spirit.

FIRST READING

From the book of the prophet Isaiah   58:1-12

Concerning fasting that pleases God

    Thus says the Lord God:
Cry out full-throated and unsparingly,
    lift up your voice like a trumpet blast;
Tell my people their wickedness,
    and the house of Jacob their sins.

They seek me day after day,
    and desire to know my ways,
Like a nation that has done what is just
    and not abandoned the law of their God;
They ask me to declare what is due them,
    pleased to gain access to God.
"Why do we fast, and you do not see it?
    afflict ourselves, and you take no note of it?"

Lo, on your fast day you carry out your own pursuits,
    and drive all your laborers.
Yes, your fast ends in quarreling and fighting,
    striking with wicked claw.
Would that today you might fast
    so as to make your voice heard on high!

49

Is this the manner fasting I wish,
   of keeping a day penance:
That a man bow head like a reed,
   and lie in sackth and ashes?
Do you call this ast,
   a day acceptab to the Lord?

This, rather, is the fasting that I wish:
   releasing those iould unjustly,
   untying the thongs of the yoke;
Setting free the oppressed,
   breaking every yoke;
Sharing your bread with the hungry,
   sheltering the oppressed and the homeless;
Clothing the naked when you see them,
   and not turning your back on your own.

Then your light shall break forth like the dawn,
   and your wound shall quickly be healed;
Your vindication shall go before you,
   and the glory of the Lord shall be your rear guard.
Then you shall call, and the Lord will answer,
   you shall cry for help, and he will say: Here I am!

If you remove from your midst oppression,
   false accusation and malicious speech;
If you bestow your bread on the hungry
   and satisfy the afflicted;
Then light shall rise for you in the darkness,
   and the gloom shall become for you like midday;

Then the Lord will guide you always
   and give you plenty even on the parched land.
    will renew your strength,
   ad you shall be like a watered garden,
    a spring whose water never fails.

The ancient ruins shall be rebuilt for your sake,
    and the foundations from ages past you shall raise up;
"Repairer of the breach," they shall call you,
    "Restorer of ruined homesteads."

RESPONSORY   Isaiah 58:6, 7, 9; Matthew 25:31, 34, 35

The Lord says: The kind of fast that pleases me
is sharing your food with the hungry
and sheltering the poor and homeless.
— Do this and I will listen to your prayers;
when you call on me I will say: I am here.

When the Son of Man comes in glory,
he will say to those on his right:
Come, inherit the kingdom,
for I was hungry and you gave me food.
— Do this and . . .

SECOND READING

From a letter to the Corinthians by Saint Clement, pope

(Cap. 7, 4—8, 3; 8, 5—9, 1; 13, 1-4; 19, 2: Funk 1, 71-73. 77-78.
87)

Repent

Let us fix our attention on the blood of Christ and
recognize how precious it is to God his Father, since it
was shed for our salvation and brought the grace of repentance to all the world.

If we review the various ages of history, we will see
that in every generation the Lord has *offered the opportunity of repentance* to any who were willing to turn to
him. When Noah preached God's message of repentance,
all who listened to him were saved. Jonah told the Nine-
vites they were going to be destroyed, but when they
repented, their prayers gained God's forgiveness for their

sins, and they were saved, even though they were not of God's people.

Under the inspiration of the Holy Spirit, the ministers of God's grace have spoken of repentance; indeed, the Master of the whole universe himself spoke of repentance with an oath: *As I live,* says the Lord, *I do not wish the death of the sinner but his repentance.* He added this evidence of his goodness: *House of Israel, repent of your wickedness. Tell the sons of my people: If their sins should reach from earth to heaven, if they are brighter than scarlet and blacker than sackcloth, you need only turn to me with your whole heart and say, "Father," and I will listen to you as to a holy people.*

In other words, God wanted all his beloved ones to have the opportunity to repent and he confirmed this desire by his own almighty will. That is why we should obey his sovereign and glorious will and prayerfully entreat his mercy and kindness. We should be suppliant before him and turn to his compassion, rejecting empty works and quarreling and jealousy which only lead to death.

Brothers, we should be humble in mind, putting aside all arrogance, pride and foolish anger. Rather, we should act in accordance with the Scriptures, as the Holy Spirit says: *The wise man must not glory in his wisdom nor the strong man in his strength nor the rich man in his riches. Rather, let him who glories glory in the Lord by seeking him and doing what is right and just.* Recall especially what the Lord Jesus said when he taught gentleness and forebearance. *Be merciful,* he said, *so that you may have mercy shown to you. Forgive, so that you may be forgiven. As you treat others, so you will be treated. As you give, so you will receive. As you judge, so you will be judged. As you are kind to others, so you*

*will be treated kindly. The measure of your giving will
be the measure of your receiving.*

Let these commandments and precepts strengthen us
to live in humble obedience to his sacred words. As
Scripture asks: *Whom shall I look upon with favor except the humble, peaceful man who trembles at my
words?*

Sharing then in the heritage of so many vast and
glorious achievements, let us hasten toward the goal of
peace, set before us from the beginning. Let us keep our
eyes firmly fixed on the Father and Creator of the whole
universe, and hold fast to his splendid and transcendent
gifts of peace and all his blessings.

RESPONSORY   Is. 55:7; Jl. 2:13; see Ez. 33:11

Let the evil man give up his way of life,
and the sinful man his thoughts.
Let him turn back to the Lord,
and the Lord will have mercy on him.
— Our God is kind and compassionate,
always ready to forgive.

The Lord does not wish the sinner to die,
but to turn back to him and live.
— Our God is . . .

Prayer, as in Morning Prayer.

Morning Prayer

Psalms and canticle, with their antiphons, may be taken from
Friday, Week III, **1459.**

READING   Deuteronomy 7:6, 8-9

You are a people sacred to the Lord, your God;
has chosen you from all the nations on the face of

earth to be a people peculiarly his own. It was because the Lord loved you and because of his fidelity to the oath he had sworn to your fathers, that he brought you out with his strong hand from the place of slavery, and ransomed you from the hand of Pharaoh, king of Egypt. Understand, then, that the Lord, your God, is God indeed, the faithful God who keeps his merciful covenant down to the thousandth generation toward those who love him and keep his commandments.

RESPONSORY

God himself will set me free, from the hunter's snare.
—God himself will set me free, from the hunter's snare.

From those who would trap me with lying words
— and from the hunter's snare.

Glory to the Father . . .
—God himself will . . .

CANTICLE OF ZECHARIAH

Ant.   When you fast, do not put on a gloomy face, like the hypocrites.

INTERCESSIONS

Today God our Father brings us to the beginning of Lent. We pray that in this time of salvation he will fill us with the Holy Spirit, purify our hearts, and strengthen us in love. Let us humbly ask him:
   Lord, give us your Holy Spirit.
May we be filled and satisfied,
—by the word which you give us.
Teach us to be loving not only in great and exceptional moments,
—but above all in the ordinary events of daily life.

May we abstain from what we do not really need,
— and help our brothers and sisters in distress.
May we bear the wounds of your Son in our bodies,
— for through his body he gave us life.
Our Father . . .

Prayer

Lord,
protect us in our struggle against evil.
As we begin the discipline of Lent,
make this day holy by our self-denial.
Grant this through our Lord Jesus Christ, your Son,
who lives and reigns with you and the Holy Spirit,
one God for ever and ever.

Daytime Prayer

Midmorning

Ant.   The time of penance has come, the time to atone
for our sins and to seek our salvation.

READING   Ezekiel 18:30b-32

Turn and be converted from all your crimes, that
they may be no cause of guilt for you. Cast away from
you all the crimes you have committed, and make for
yourselves a new heart and a new spirit. Why should you
die, O house of Israel? For I have no pleasure in the
death of anyone who dies, says the Lord God. Return
and live!

Create a clean heart in me, O God.
— Renew in me a steadfast spirit.

Midday

Ant.   As I live, says the Lord, I do not wish the si'
to die but to turn back to me and live.

READING   Zechariah 1:3b-4b

Return to me, says the Lord of hosts, and I will return to you, says the Lord of hosts. Be not like your
fathers whom the former prophets warned: Turn from
your evil ways and your wicked deeds.

Turn your face away from my sins.
— Blot out all my guilt.

Midafternoon

Ant.   Armed with God's justice and power, let us prove
        ourselves through patient endurance.

READING   Daniel 4:24b

Atone for your sins by good deeds, and for your misdeeds by kindness to the poor; then your prosperity will
be long.

My sacrifice to God is a contrite spirit.
— A humble, contrite heart, O God, you will not spurn.

Prayer, as in Morning Prayer.

Evening Prayer

READING   Philippians 2:12b-15a

Work with anxious concern to achieve your salvation.
It is God who, in his good will toward you, begets in
you any measure of desire or achievement. In everything
you do, act without grumbling or arguing; prove yourselves innocent and straightforward, children of God
beyond reproach.

RESPONSORY

you, O Lord, I make my prayer for mercy.
        you, O Lord, I make my prayer for mercy.

Heal my soul, for I have sinned against you.
— I make my prayer for mercy.

Glory to the Father . . .
— To you, O Lord . . .

CANTICLE OF MARY

Ant. When you give alms, do not let your left hand
know what your right hand is doing.

INTERCESSIONS

All glory and honor to God, for in the blood of Christ he
has ratified a new and everlasting covenant with his
people, and renews it in the sacrament of the altar.
Let us lift our voices in prayer:
Bless your people, Lord.
Lord, guide the minds and hearts of peoples and all
in public office,
— may they seek the common good.
Renew the spirit of dedication in those who have left all
to follow Christ,
— may they give clear witness to the holiness of the
Church.
You have made all men and women in your image,
— may they always uphold human dignity.
Lead back to your friendship and truth all who have
gone astray,
— teach us how to help them.
Grant that the dead may enter into your glory,
— to praise you for ever.

Our Father . . .

Prayer
Lord,
protect us in our struggle against evil.

As we begin the discipline of Lent,
make this day holy by our self-denial.

Grant this through our Lord Jesus Christ, your Son,
who lives and reigns with you and the Holy Spirit,
one God, for ever and ever.

THURSDAY AFTER ASH WEDNESDAY

Office of Readings

Whoever meditates on the law of the Lord.
— Will bring forth much fruit at harvest time.

FIRST READING

From the beginning of the book of Exodus   1:1-22

The oppression of Israel

These are the names of the sons of Israel who, ac-
companied by their households, migrated with Jacob into
Egypt: Reuben, Simeon, Levi and Judah; Issachar, Zeb-
ulun and Benjamin; Dan and Naphtali; Gad and Asher.
The total number of the direct descendants of Jacob was
seventy. Joseph was already in Egypt.

Now Joseph and all his brothers and that whole generation died. But the Israelites were fruitful and prolific.
They became so numerous and strong that the land was
filled with them.

Then a new king, who knew nothing of Joseph, came
to power in Egypt. He said to his subjects, "Look how
numerous and powerful the Israelite people are growing,
more so than we ourselves! Come, let us deal shrewdly
with them to stop their increase; otherwise, in time of
war they too may join our enemies to fight against us,
and so leave our country."

Accordingly, taskmasters were set over the Israelites
to oppress them with forced labor. Thus they had to
build for Pharaoh the supply cities of Pithom and Raam-
ses. Yet the more they were oppressed, the more they
multiplied and spread. The Egyptians, then, dreaded the
Israelites and reduced them to cruel slavery, making life
bitter for them with hard work in mortar and brick and
all kinds of field work—the whole cruel fate of slaves.

The king of Egypt told the Hebrew midwives, one of
whom was called Shiphrah and the other Puah, "When
you act as midwives for the Hebrew women and see
them giving birth, if it is a boy, kill him, but if it is a
girl, she may live." The midwives, however, feared God;
they did not do as the king of Egypt had ordered them,
but let the boys live.

So the king summoned the midwives and asked them,
"Why have you acted thus, allowing the boys to live?"
The midwives answered Pharaoh, "The Hebrew women
are not like the Egyptian women. They are robust and
give birth before the midwife arrives." Therefore God
dealt well with the midwives. The people, too, increased
and grew strong. And because the midwives feared God,
he built up families for them.

Pharaoh then commanded all his subjects, "Throw
into the river every boy that is born to the Hebrews, but
you may let all the girls live."

RESPONSORY   Genesis 15:13-14; Isaiah 49:26

The Lord said to Abraham: Know this for certain;
your children will be exiles in a land not their own,
enslaved and oppressed for four hundred years.
— Then I will punish the nation that enslaved them.

I am the Lord, your Savior and Redeemer.
— Then I will . . .

SECOND READING

From a sermon by Saint Leo the Great, pope

(Sermo 6 de Quadragesima, 1-2: PL 54, 285-287)

Purification of spirit through fasting and almsgiving

Dear friends, at every moment *the earth is full of the mercy of God*, and nature itself is a lesson for all the faithful in the worship of God. The heavens, the sea and all that is in them bear witness to the goodness and omnipotence of their Creator, and the marvelous beauty of the elements as they obey him demands from the intelligent creation a fitting expression of its gratitude.

But with the return of that season marked out in a special way by the mystery of our redemption, and of the days that lead up to the paschal feast, we are summoned more urgently to prepare ourselves by a purification of spirit.

The special note of the paschal feast is this: the whole Church rejoices in the forgiveness of sins. It rejoices in the forgiveness not only of those who are then reborn in holy baptism but also of those who are already numbered among God's adopted children.

Initially, men are made new by the rebirth of baptism. Yet there is still required a daily renewal to repair the shortcomings of our mortal nature, and whatever degree of progress has been made there is no one who should not be more advanced. All must therefore strive to ensure that on the day of redemption no one may be found in the sins of his former life.

Dear friends, what the Christian should be doing at all times should be done now with greater care and devotion, so that the Lenten fast enjoined by the apostles may be fulfilled, not simply by abstinence from food but above all by the renunciation of sin.

There is no more profitable practice as a companion to holy and spiritual fasting than that of almsgiving. This embraces under the single name of mercy many excellent works of devotion, so that the good intentions of all the faithful may be of equal value, even where their means are not. The love that we owe both God and man is always free from any obstacle that would prevent us from having a good intention. The angels sang: *Glory to God in the highest, and peace to his people on earth.* The person who shows love and compassion to those in any kind of affliction is blessed, not only with the virtue of good will but also with the gift of peace.

The works of mercy are innumerable. Their very variety brings this advantage to those who are true Christians, that in the matter of almsgiving not only the rich and affluent but also those of average means and the poor are able to play their part. Those who are unequal in their capacity to give can be equal in the love within their hearts.

RESPONSORY

This time of fasting opens the gates of heaven to us. Let us welcome it and pray
— that when Easter comes
we may share the joy of the risen Lord.

In all we do let us show
that we are the servants of God.
— That when Easter . . .

Prayer, as in Morning Prayer.

Morning Prayer

READING　　　　　　　　　　See 1 Kings 8:51-53a

We are your people and your inheritance, O Lord. May your eyes be open to the petition of your servant and to the petition of your people Israel. Hear us whenever we call upon you, because you have set us apart among all the peoples of the earth for your inheritance.

RESPONSORY

God himself will set me free, from the hunter's snare.
— God himself will set me free, from the hunter's snare.

From those who would trap me with lying words
— and from the hunter's snare.

Glory to the Father . . .
— God himself will . . .

CANTICLE OF ZECHARIAH

Ant.　If anyone wishes to be my disciple, he must deny himself, take up his cross, and follow me, says the Lord.

INTERCESSIONS

God has revealed himself in Christ. Let us praise his goodness, and ask him from our hearts:
　　Remember us, Lord, for we are your children.
Teach us to enter more deeply into the mystery of the Church,
— that it may be more effective for ourselves and for the world as the sacrament of salvation.
Lover of mankind, inspire us to work for human progress,
— seeking to spread your kingdom in all we do.

May our hearts thirst for Christ,
— the fountain of living water.
Forgive us our sins,
— and direct our steps into the ways of justice and
  sincerity.

Our Father . . .

Prayer

Lord,
may everything we do
begin with your inspiration,
continue with your help,
and reach perfection under your guidance.

We ask this through our Lord Jesus Christ, your Son,
who lives and reigns with you and the Holy Spirit,
one God, for ever and ever.

Daytime Prayer

Midmorning

Ant. The time of penance has come, the time to atone
      for our sins and to seek our salvation.

READING   Isaiah 55:6-7

Seek the Lord while he may be found,
   call him while he is near.
Let the scoundrel forsake his way,
   and the wicked man his thoughts;
Let him turn to the Lord for mercy;
   to our God, who is generous in forgiving.

Create a clean heart in me, O God.
— Renew in me a steadfast spirit.

Midday

Ant. As I live, says the Lord, I do not wish the sinner to die but to turn back to me and live.

READING Deuteronomy 30:2-3a

Provided that you and your children return to the Lord, your God, and heed his voice with all your heart and with all your soul, just as I now command you, the Lord, your God, will change your lot; and taking pity on you, he will again gather you from all the nations.

Turn your face away from my sins.
— Blot out all my guilt.

Midafternoon

Ant. Armed with God's justice and power, let us prove ourselves through patient endurance.

READING Hebrews 10:35-36

Do not surrender your confidence; it will have great reward. You need patience to do God's will and receive what he has promised.

My sacrifice to God is a contrite spirit.
—A humble, contrite heart, O God, you will not spurn.

Prayer, as in Morning Prayer.

Evening Prayer

READING James 4:7-8, 10

Submit to God; resist the devil and he will take flight. Draw close to God, and he will draw close to you. Cleanse your hands, you sinners; purify your hearts, you backsliders. Be humbled in the sight of the Lord and he will raise you on high.

RESPONSORY

To you, O Lord, I make my prayer for mercy.
— To you, O Lord, I make my prayer for mercy.

Heal my soul, for I have sinned against you.
— I make my prayer for mercy.

Glory to the Father . . .
— To you, O Lord . . .

CANTICLE OF MARY

Ant. Whoever gives up his life for my sake in this
      world will find it again for ever in the next, says
      the Lord.

INTERCESSIONS

In his mercy, God sends the Holy Spirit to shine on us,
    so that our lives may radiate holiness and faith. Let
    us raise our voices in prayer and say:
    *Lord, give life to your people, whom Christ has re-
    deemed.*
Lord, source of all holiness, draw bishops, priests and
    deacons closer to Christ through the eucharistic
    mystery,
— may they grow daily in the grace of their ordination.
Teach Christ's faithful people to be devout and attentive
    at the table of his word and of his body,
— so that they may bring into their daily lives the grace
    they receive through faith and sacrament.
Grant, Lord, that we may see in each person the dignity
    of one redeemed by your Son's blood,
— so that we may respect the freedom and the con-
    science of all.
Teach us to restrain our greed for earthly goods,
— and to have concern for the needs of others.

Be merciful to your faithful people whom you have
   called to yourself today,
— grant them the gift of eternal happiness.

Our Father . . .

Prayer

Lord,
may everything we do
begin with your inspiration,
continue with your help,
and reach perfection under your guidance.
We ask this through our Lord Jesus Christ, your Son,
who lives and reigns with you and the Holy Spirit,
one God, for ever and ever.

FRIDAY AFTER ASH WEDNESDAY

Office of Readings

Turn back to the Lord your God.
— He is kind and merciful.

First Reading

From the book of Exodus   2:1-22; 18:4

The birth and flight of Moses

A certain man of the house of Levi married a Levite
woman, who conceived and bore a son. Seeing that he
was a goodly child, she hid him for three months. When
she could hide him no longer, she took a papyrus basket,
daubed it with bitumen and pitch, and putting the child
in it, placed it among the reeds on the river bank. His
sister stationed herself at a distance to find out what
would happen to him.

Pharaoh's daughter came down to the river to bathe, while her maids walked along the river bank. Noticing the basket among the reeds, she sent her handmaid to fetch it. On opening it, she looked, and lo, there was a baby boy, crying! She was moved with pity for him and said, "It is one of the Hebrews' children." Then his sister asked Pharaoh's daughter, "Shall I go and call one of the Hebrew women to nurse the child for you?" "Yes, do so," she answered.

So the maiden went and called the child's own mother. Pharaoh's daughter said to her, "Take this child and nurse it for me, and I will repay you." The woman therefore took the child and nursed it. When the child grew, she brought him to Pharaoh's daughter, who adopted him as her son and called him Moses; for she said, "I drew him out of the water."

On one occasion, after Moses had grown up, when he visited his kinsmen and witnessed their forced labor, he saw an Egyptian striking a Hebrew, one of his own kinsmen. Looking about and seeing no one, he slew the Egyptian and hid him in the sand. The next day he went out again, and now two Hebrews were fighting! So he asked the culprit, "Why are you striking your fellow Hebrew?" But he replied, "Who has appointed you ruler and judge over us? Are you thinking of killing me as you killed the Egyptian?" Then Moses became afraid and thought, "The affair must certainly be known."

Pharaoh, too, heard of the affair and sought to put him to death. But Moses fled from him and stayed in the land of Midian. As he was seated there by a well, seven daughters of a priest of Midian came to draw water and fill the troughs to water their father's flock. But some shepherds came and drove them away. Then Moses got up and defended them and watered their flock.

When they returned to their father Reuel, he said to them, "How is it you have returned so soon today?" They answered, "An Egyptian saved us from the interference of the shepherds. He even drew water for us and watered the flock!" "Where is the man?" he asked his daughters. "Why did you leave him there? Invite him to have something to eat."

Moses agreed to live with him, and the man gave him his daughter Zipporah in marriage. She bore him a son, whom he named Gershom; for he said, "I am a stranger in a foreign land." The other son she bore was called Eliezer; for he said, "My father's God is my helper; he has rescued me from Pharaoh's sword."

RESPONSORY   Hebrews 11:24-25, 26, 27

When he grew up, Moses, guided by faith,
refused to be known as the son of Pharaoh's daughter.
He chose to suffer with the people of God
rather than have the fleeting pleasures of sin.
— He fixed his gaze on the reward God had promised.

To bear the stigma of Christ was worth more to him
than all the treasures of Egypt.
With faith as his guide he left Egypt behind.
— He fixed his . . .

SECOND READING

From a homily by Saint John Chrysostom, bishop

(Supp., Hom. 6 De precatione: PG 64, 462-466)

Prayer is the light of the spirit

Prayer and converse with God is a supreme good: it is a partnership and union with God. As the eyes of the body are enlightened when they see light, so our spirit, when it is intent on God, is illumined by his infinite light.

I do not mean the prayer of outward observance but prayer from the heart, not confined to fixed times or periods but continuous throughout the day and night.

Our spirit should be quick to reach out toward God, not only when it is engaged in meditation; at other times also, when it is carrying out its duties, caring for the needy, performing works of charity, giving generously in the service of others, our spirit should long for God and call him to mind, so that these works may be seasoned with the salt of God's love, and so make a palatable offering to the Lord of the universe. Throughout the whole of our lives we may enjoy the benefit that comes from prayer if we devote a great deal of time to it.

Prayer is the light of the spirit, true knowledge of God, mediating between God and man. The spirit, raised up to heaven by prayer, clings to God with the utmost tenderness; like a child crying tearfully for its mother, it craves the milk that God provides. It seeks the satisfaction of its own desires, and receives gifts outweighing the whole world of nature.

Prayer stands before God as an honored ambassador. It gives joy to the spirit, peace to the heart. I speak of prayer, not words. It is the longing for God, love too deep for words, a gift not given by man but by God's grace. The apostle Paul says: *We do not know how we are to pray but the Spirit himself pleads for us with inexpressible longings.*

When the Lord gives this kind of prayer to a man, he gives him riches that cannot be taken away, heavenly food that satisfies the spirit. One who tastes this food is set on fire with an eternal longing for the Lord: his spirit burns as in a fire of the utmost intensity.

Practice prayer from the beginning. Paint your house with the colors of modesty and humility. Make it radiant

with the light of justice. Decorate it with the finest gold
leaf of good deeds. Adorn it with the walls and stones of
faith and generosity. Crown it with the pinnacle of
prayer. In this way you will make it a perfect dwelling
place for the Lord. You will be able to receive him as in
a splendid palace, and through his grace you will already
possess him, his image enthroned in the temple of your
spirit.

RESPONSORY   Lamentations 5:20; Matthew 8:25

Will you forget us for ever?
Will you leave us abandoned day after day?
— Turn us back to you, O Lord,
and we will come to you.

Save us, Lord, or we shall perish.
— Turn us back . . .

Prayer, as in Morning Prayer.

Morning Prayer

READING   Isaiah 53:11b-12

Through his suffering, my servant shall justify many,
    and their guilt he shall bear.
Therefore I will give him his portion among the great,
    and he shall divide the spoils with the mighty,
Because he surrendered himself to death
    and was counted among the wicked:
And he shall take away the sins of many,
    and win pardon for their offenses.

RESPONSORY

God himself will set me free, from the hunter's snare.
— God himself will set me free, from the hunter's snare.

From those who would trap me with lying words
—and from the hunter's snare.

Glory to the Father . . .
—God himself will . . .

CANTICLE OF ZECHARIAH

Ant. When you meet those who are in need of clothing,
do not turn away from them, for they are your
brothers. Then your light shall break forth like
the dawn, and your good deeds shall go before
you.

INTERCESSIONS

Let us pray to Christ our Savior, who redeemed us by
his death and resurrection:
Lord, have mercy on us.
You went up to Jerusalem to suffer and so enter into
your glory,
—bring your Church to the Passover feast of heaven.
You were lifted high on the cross and pierced by the
soldier's lance,
—heal our wounds.
You made the cross the tree of life,
—give its fruit to those reborn in baptism.
On the cross you forgave the repentant thief,
—forgive us our sins.

Our Father . . .

Prayer

Lord,
with your loving care
guide the penance we have begun.
Help us to persevere with love and sincerity.

Grant this through our Lord Jesus Christ, your Son,
who lives and reigns with you and the Holy Spirit,
one God, for ever and ever.

Daytime Prayer
Midmorning

Ant.   The time of penance has come, the time to atone
for our sins and to seek our salvation.

READING   Isaiah 55:3

Come to me heedfully,
listen, that you may have life.
I will renew with you the everlasting covenant,
the benefits assured to David.

Create a clean heart in me, O God.
— Renew in me a steadfast spirit.

Midday

Ant.   As I live, says the Lord, I do not wish the sinner
to die but to turn back to me and live.

READING   See Jeremiah 3:12b, 14a

Return, says the Lord,
I will not remain angry with you;
For I am merciful,
I will not continue my wrath forever.
Return, rebellious children, says the Lord.

Turn your face away from my sins.
— Blot out all my guilt.

Midafternoon

Ant.   Armed with God's justice and power, let us prove
ourselves through patient endurance.

READING   James 1:27

Looking after orphans and widows in their distress and keeping oneself unspotted by the world make for pure worship without stain before our God and Father.

My sacrifice to God is a contrite spirit.
—A humble, contrite heart, O God, you will not spurn.

Prayer, as in Morning Prayer.

Evening Prayer

READING   James 5:16, 19-20

Declare your sins to one another, and pray for one another, that you may find healing. The fervent petition of a holy man is powerful indeed. My brothers, the case may arise among you of someone straying from the truth, and of another bringing him back. Remember this: the person who brings a sinner back from his way will save his soul from death and cancel a multitude of sins.

RESPONSORY

To you, O Lord, I make my prayer for mercy.
— To you, O Lord, I make my prayer for mercy.

Heal my soul, for I have sinned against you.
— I make my prayer for mercy.

Glory to the Father . . .
— To you, O Lord . . .

CANTICLE OF MARY

Ant. When the bridegroom is taken away from them, then will be the time for the wedding guests to fast.

INTERCESSIONS

The Savior of mankind by dying destroyed death and
    by rising again restored life. Let us humbly ask him:
    Sanctify your people, redeemed by your blood.

Redeemer of the world, give us a greater share of your
    passion through a deeper spirit of repentance,
— so that we may share the glory of your resurrection.

May your Mother, comfort of the afflicted, protect us,
— may we console others as you console us.

In their trials enable your faithful people to share in
    your passion,
— and so reveal in their lives your saving power.

You humbled yourself by being obedient even to accept-
    ing death, death on a cross,
— give all who serve you the gifts of obedience and
    patient endurance.

Transform the bodies of the dead to be like your own in
    glory,
— and bring us at last into their fellowship.

Our Father . . .

Prayer

Lord,
with your loving care
guide the penance we have begun.
Help us to persevere with love and sincerity.

Grant this through our Lord Jesus Christ, your Son,
who lives and reigns with you and the Holy Spirit,
one God, for ever and ever.

SATURDAY AFTER ASH WEDNESDAY

Office of Readings

The man of God welcomes the light.
— So that all may see that his deeds are true.

FIRST READING

From the book of Exodus   3:1-20

The call of Moses and the revelation of the Lord's name

Moses was tending the flock of his father-in-law Jethro, the priest of Midian. Leading the flock across the desert, he came to Horeb, the mountain of God. There an angel of the Lord appeared to him in fire flaming out of a bush. As he looked on, he was surprised to see that the bush, though on fire, was not consumed. So Moses decided, "I must go over to look at this remarkable sight, and see why the bush is not burned."

When the Lord saw him coming over to look at it more closely, God called out to him from the bush, "Moses! Moses!" He answered, "Here I am." God said, "Come no nearer! Remove the sandals from your feet, for the place where you stand is holy ground. I am the God of your father," he continued, "the God of Abraham, the God of Isaac, the God of Jacob." Moses hid his face, for he was afraid to look at God.

But the Lord said, "I have witnessed the affliction of my people in Egypt and have heard their cry of complaint against their slave drivers, so I know well what they are suffering. Therefore I have come down to rescue them from the hands of the Egyptians and lead them out of that land into a good and spacious land, a land flowing with milk and honey, the country of the Canaanites,

Hittites, Amorites, Perizzites, Hivites and Jebusites. So indeed the cry of the Israelites has reached me, and I have truly noted that the Egyptians are oppressing them. Come, now! I will send you to Pharaoh to lead my people, the Israelites, out of Egypt."

But Moses said to God, "Who am I that I should go to Pharaoh and lead the Israelites out of Egypt?" He answered, "I will be with you; and this shall be your proof that it is I who have sent you: when you bring my people out of Egypt, you will worship God on this very mountain."

"But," said Moses to God, "when I go to the Israelites and say to them, 'The God of your fathers has sent me to you,' if they ask me, 'What is his name?' what am I to tell them?" God replied, "I am who am." Then he added, "This is what you shall tell the Israelites: I AM sent me to you."

God spoke further to Moses, "Thus shall you say to the Israelites: The Lord, the God of your fathers, the God of Abraham, the God of Isaac, the God of Jacob, has sent me to you.

"This is my name forever;
    this is my title for all generations.

"Go and assemble the elders of the Israelites, and tell them: The Lord, the God of your fathers, the God of Abraham, Isaac and Jacob, has appeared to me and said: I am concerned about you and about the way you are being treated in Egypt; so I have decided to lead you up out of the misery of Egypt into the land of the Canaanites, Hittites, Amorites, Perizzites, Hivites and Jebusites, a land flowing with milk and honey.

"Thus they will heed your message. Then you and the elders of Israel shall go to the king of Egypt and say to him: The Lord, the God of the Hebrews, has sent us word. Permit us, then, to go a three-days' journey in the desert, that we may offer sacrifice to the Lord, our God.

"Yet I know that the king of Egypt will not allow you to go unless he is forced. I will stretch out my hand, therefore, and smite Egypt by doing all kinds of wondrous deeds there. After that he will send you away."

RESPONSORY   Exodus 3:14; Isaiah 43:11

God said to Moses: I am who am.
— Tell the people of Israel: I AM sent me to you.

I, and I alone, am the Lord;
there is no other who can save you.
— Tell the people . . .

SECOND READING

From the treatise Against Heresies by Saint Irenaeus, bishop

(Lib. 4, 13, 4—14, 1: SC 100, 534-540)

The friendship of God

Our Lord, the Word of God, first drew men to God as servants, but later he freed those made subject to him. He himself testified to this: *I do not call you servants any longer, for a servant does not know what his master is doing. Instead I call you friends, since I have made known to you everything that I have learned from my Father.* Friendship with God brings the gift of immortality to those who accept it.

In the beginning God created Adam, not because he needed man, but because he wanted to have someone on whom to bestow his blessings. Not only before Adam but also before all creation, the Word was glorifying the Father in whom he dwelt, and was himself being glorified by the Father. The Word himself said: *Father, glorify me with that glory that I had with you before the world was.*

Nor did the Lord need our service. He commanded us to follow him, but his was the gift of salvation. To follow the Savior is to share in salvation; to follow the light is to enjoy the light. Those who are in the light do not illuminate the light but are themselves illuminated and enlightened by the light. They add nothing to the light; rather, they are beneficiaries, for they are enlightened by the light.

The same is true of service to God: it adds nothing to God, nor does God need the service of man. Rather, he gives life and immortality and eternal glory to those who follow and serve him. He confers a benefit on his servants in return for their service and on his followers in return for their loyalty, but he receives no benefit from them. He is rich, perfect and in need of nothing.

The reason why God requires service from man is this: because he is good and merciful he desires to confer benefits on those who persevere in his service. In proportion to God's need of nothing is man's need for communion with God.

This is the glory of man: to persevere and remain in the service of God. For this reason the Lord told his disciples: *You did not choose me but I chose you.* He meant that his disciples did not glorify him by following him, but in following the Son of God they were glorified by him. As he said: *I wish that where I am they also may be, that they may see my glory.*

RESPONSORY   Deuteronomy 10:12; Matthew 22:38

This is what the Lord God asks of you:
— to fear him, and to love and serve him
with all your heart and soul.

This is the first and the greatest commandment:
— To fear him . . .

Prayer, as in Morning Prayer.

Morning Prayer

READING   Isaiah 1: 16-18

Wash yourselves clean!
Put away your misdeeds from before my eyes;
    cease doing evil; learn to do good.
Make justice your aim; redress the wronged,
    hear the orphan's plea, defend the widow.
Come now, let us set things right,
    says the Lord:
Though your sins be like scarlet,
    they may become white as snow;
Though they be crimson red,
    they may become white as wool.

RESPONSORY

God himself will set me free, from the hunter's snare.
— God himself will set me free, from the hunter's snare.

From those who would trap me with lying words
— and from the hunter's snare.

Glory to the Father . . .
— God himself will . . .

CANTICLE OF ZECHARIAH

Ant.   Store up for yourselves treasures in heaven where
        neither rust nor moth can destroy.

INTERCESSIONS

Let us always and everywhere give thanks to Christ our
    Savior, and ask him with confidence:
    Lord, help us with your grace.
May we keep our bodies pure,
— as temples of the Holy Spirit.
May we offer ourselves this morning to the service of
    others,
— and do your will in all things throughout the day.
Teach us to seek the bread of everlasting life,
— the bread that is your gift.
May your Mother, the refuge of sinners, pray for us,
— and gain for us your loving forgiveness.

Our Father . . .

Prayer

Father,
look upon our weakness
and reach out to help us with your loving power.

We ask this through our Lord Jesus Christ, your Son,
who lives and reigns with you and the Holy Spirit,
one God, for ever and ever.

Daytime Prayer

Midmorning

Ant.   The time of penance has come, the time to atone
        for our sins and to seek our salvation.

READING   Revelation 3:19-20

Whoever is dear to me I reprove and chastise. Be
earnest about it, therefore. Repent! Here I stand, knock-
ing at the door. If anyone hears me calling and opens

the door, I will enter his house and have supper with him, and he with me.

Create a clean heart in me, O God.
— Renew in me a steadfast spirit.

Midday

Ant.   As I live, says the Lord, I do not wish the sinner
        to die but to turn back to me and live.

READING   Isaiah 44:21-22

Remember this,
    you who are my servant!
I formed you to be a servant to me;
    O Israel, by me you shall never be forgotten:
I have brushed away your offenses like a cloud,
    your sins like a mist;
    return to me, for I have redeemed you.

Turn your face away from my sins.
— Blot out all my guilt.

Midafternoon

Ant.   Armed with God's justice and power, let us prove
        ourselves through patient endurance.

READING   Galatians 6:7b-8

No one makes a fool of God! A man will reap only what he sows. If he sows in the field of the flesh, he will reap a harvest of corruption; but if his seed-ground is the spirit, he will reap everlasting life.

My sacrifice to God is a contrite spirit.
— A humble, contrite heart, O God, you will not spurn.

Prayer, as in Morning Prayer.

FIRST SUNDAY OF LENT

Psalter, Week I

Evening Prayer I

Hymn, 33.

Ant. 1   Lord God, we ask you to receive us and be pleased with the sacrifice we offer you this day with humble and contrite hearts.

Psalms and canticle from Sunday, Week I, 1076.

Ant. 2   Call upon the Lord and he will hear you; cry out and he will answer: Here I am.

Ant. 3   Christ died for our sins, the innocent for the guilty, to bring us back to God. In the body he was put to death, but in the spirit he was raised to life.

READING   2 Corinthians 6:1-4a

We beg you not to receive the grace of God in vain. For he says, "In an acceptable time I have heard you; on a day of salvation I have helped you." Now is the acceptable time! Now is the day of salvation! We avoid giving anyone offense, so that our ministry may not be blamed. On the contrary, in all that we do we strive to present ourselves as ministers of God.

RESPONSORY

Listen to us, O Lord, and have mercy, for we have sinned against you.
—Listen to us, O Lord, and have mercy, for we have sinned against you.

Christ Jesus, hear our humble petitions,
—for we have sinned against you.

Glory to the Father . . .
— Listen to us . . .

CANTICLE OF MARY

Ant. Man cannot live on bread alone but by every
word that comes from the mouth of God.

INTERCESSIONS

Let us give glory to Christ the Lord, who became our
teacher and example and our brother. Let us pray to
him, saying:
Lord, fill your people with your life.
Lord Jesus, you became like us in all things but sin;
teach us how to share with others their joy and sorrow,
— that our love may grow deeper every day.
Help us to feed you in feeding the hungry,
— and to give you drink in giving drink to the thirsty.
You raised Lazarus from the sleep of death,
— grant that those who have died the death of sin may
rise again through faith and repentance.
Inspire many to follow you with greater zeal and perfection,
— through the example of the blessed Virgin Mary and
the saints.
Let the dead rise in your glory,
— to enjoy your love for ever.

Our Father . . .

Prayer

Father,
through our observance of Lent,
help us to understand the meaning
of your Son's death and resurrection,
and teach us to reflect it in our lives.

Grant this through our Lord Jesus Christ, your Son,
who lives and reigns with you and the Holy Spirit,
one God, for ever and ever.

Alternative Prayer

Lord our God,
you formed man from the clay of the earth
and breathed into him the spirit of life,
but he turned from your face and sinned.
In this time of repentance
we call out for your mercy.
Bring us back to you
and to the life your Son won for us
by his death on the cross,
for he lives and reigns for ever and ever.

Office of Readings

Man cannot live on bread alone.
—But by every word that comes from the mouth of
   God.

FIRST READING

From the book of Exodus   5:1—6:1

The oppression of the people

Moses and Aaron went to Pharaoh and said, "Thus
says the Lord, the God of Israel: Let my people go, that
they may celebrate a feast to me in the desert." Pharaoh
answered, "Who is the Lord, that I should heed his plea
to let Israel go? I do not know the Lord; even if I did,
I would not let Israel go." They replied, "The God of
the Hebrews has sent us word. Let us go a three days'
journey in the desert, that we may offer sacrifice to the

Lord, our God; otherwise he will punish us with pestilence or the sword."

The king of Egypt answered them, "What do you mean, Moses and Aaron, by taking the people away from their work? Off to your labor! Look how numerous the people of the land are already," continued Pharaoh, "and yet you would give them rest from their labor!"

That very day Pharaoh gave the taskmasters and foremen of the people this order: "You shall no longer supply the people with straw for their brickmaking as you have previously done. Let them go and gather straw themselves! Yet you shall levy upon them the same quota of bricks as they have previously made. Do not reduce it. They are lazy; that is why they are crying, 'Let us go to offer sacrifice to our God.' Increase the work for the men, so that they keep their mind on it and pay no attention to lying words."

So the taskmasters and foremen of the people went out and told them, "Thus says Pharaoh: I will not provide you with straw. Go and gather the straw yourselves, wherever you can find it. Yet there must not be the slightest reduction in your work." The people, then, scattered throughout the land of Egypt to gather stubble for straw, while the taskmasters kept driving them on, saying, "Finish your work, the same daily amount as when your straw was supplied."

The foremen of the Israelites, whom the taskmasters of Pharaoh had placed over them, were beaten, and were asked, "Why have you not completed your prescribed amount of bricks yesterday and today, as before?"

Then the Israelite foremen came and made this appeal to Pharaoh: "Why do you treat your servants in this manner? No straw is supplied to your servants, and still we are told to make bricks. Look how your servants are beaten! It is you who are at fault." Pharaoh answered, "It is just because you are lazy that you keep saying, 'Let us go and offer sacrifice to the Lord.' Off to work, then! Straw shall not be provided for you, but you must still deliver your quota of bricks."

The Israelite foremen knew they were in a sorry plight, having been told not to reduce the daily amount of bricks. When, therefore, they left Pharaoh and came upon Moses and Aaron, who were waiting to meet them, they said to them, "The Lord look upon you and judge! You have brought us into bad odor with Pharaoh and his servants and have put a sword in their hands to slay us."

Moses again had recourse to the Lord and said, "Lord, why do you treat this people so badly? And why did you send me on such a mission? Ever since I went to Pharaoh to speak in your name, he has maltreated this people of yours, and you have done nothing to rescue them."

Then the Lord answered Moses, "Now you shall see what I will do to Pharaoh. Forced by my mighty hand, he will send them away; compelled by my outstretched arm, he will drive them from his land."

RESPONSORY   Exodus 5:1, 3

Moses stood before the Pharaoh and said:
These are the words of the Lord God of Israel:
— Let my people go,
so that they may keep a feast in my honor in the wilderness.

The Lord God of the Hebrews has sent me to you with this message:
— Let my people . . .

SECOND READING

From a commentary on the psalms by Saint Augustine, bishop

(Ps. 60, 2-3: CCL 39, 766)

> *In Christ we suffered temptation,*
> *and in him we overcame the devil*

Hear, O God, my petition, listen to my prayer. Who is speaking? An individual, it seems. See if it is an individual: *I cried to you from the ends of the earth while my heart was in anguish.* Now it is no longer one person; rather, it is one in the sense that Christ is one, and we are all his members. What single individual can cry from the ends of the earth? The one who cries from the ends of the earth is none other than the Son's inheritance. It was said to him: *Ask of me, and I shall give you the nations as your inheritance, and the ends of the earth as your possession.* This possession of Christ, this inheritance of Christ, this body of Christ, this one Church of Christ, this unity that we are, cries from the ends of the earth. What does it cry? What I said before: *Hear, O God, my petition, listen to my prayer; I cried out to you from the ends of the earth.* That is, I made this cry to you *from the ends of the earth*; that is, on all sides.

Why did I make this cry? *While my heart was in anguish.* The speaker shows that he is present among all the nations of the earth in a condition, not of exalted glory but of severe trial.

Our pilgrimage on earth cannot be exempt from trial. We progress by means of trial. No one knows himself except through trial, or receives a crown except after victory, or strives except against an enemy or temptations.

The one who cries from the ends of the earth is in anguish, but is not left on his own. Christ chose to foreshadow us, who are his body, by means of his body, in which he has died, risen and ascended into heaven, so that the members of his body may hope to follow where their head has gone before.

He made us one with him when he chose to be tempted by Satan. We have heard in the gospel how the Lord Jesus Christ was tempted by the devil in the wilderness. Certainly Christ was tempted by the devil. In Christ you were tempted, for Christ received his flesh from your nature, but by his own power gained salvation for you; he suffered death in your nature, but by his own power gained life for you; he suffered insults in your nature, but by his own power gained glory for you; therefore, he suffered temptation in your nature, but by his own power gained victory for you.

If in Christ we have been tempted, in him we overcome the devil. Do you think only of Christ's temptations and fail to think of his victory? See yourself as tempted in him, and see yourself as victorious in him. He could have kept the devil from himself; but if he were not tempted he could not teach you how to triumph over temptation.

RESPONSORY   Jeremiah 1:19; 39:18

They will fight against you, but shall not defeat you,
— for I am with you to deliver you, says the Lord.

You shall not fall by the sword;
I will keep you safe.
— For I am . . .

Prayer, as in Morning Prayer.

Morning Prayer

Hymn, 43.

Ant. 1   I will praise you all my life, O Lord; in your name I will lift up my hands.

Psalms and canticle from Sunday, Week I, 1088.

Ant. 2   Sing a hymn of praise to our God; praise him above all for ever.

Ant. 3   The Lord delights in his people; he honors the humble with victory.

Reading   See Nehemiah 8:9, 10

Today is holy to the Lord your God. Do not be sad, and do not weep; for today is holy to our Lord. Do not be saddened this day, for rejoicing in the Lord must be your strength!

Responsory

Christ, Son of the living God, have mercy on us.
— Christ, Son of the living God, have mercy on us.

You were wounded for our offenses,
— have mercy on us.

Glory to the Father . . .
— Christ, Son of . . .

Canticle of Zechariah

Ant.   Jesus was led by the Spirit into the desert to be tempted by the devil; and when he had fasted for forty days and forty nights, he was hungry.

Intercessions

Let us praise our loving Redeemer, who gained for us this season of grace, and pray to him, saying:

Lord, create a new spirit in us.

Christ, our life, through baptism we were buried with
you and rose to life with you,
— may we walk today in newness of life.

Lord, you have brought blessings to all mankind,
— bring us to share your concern for the good of all.

May we work together to build up the earthly city,
— with our eyes fixed on the city that lasts for ever.

Healer of body and soul, cure the sickness of our spirit,
— so that we may grow in holiness through your con-
stant care.

Our Father . . .

Prayer

Father,
through our observance of Lent,
help us to understand the meaning
of your Son's death and resurrection,
and teach us to reflect it in our lives.

Grant this through our Lord Jesus Christ, your Son,
who lives and reigns with you and the Holy Spirit,
one God, for ever and ever.

Alternative Prayer

Lord our God,
you formed man from the clay of the earth
and breathed into him the spirit of life,
but he turned from your face and sinned.
In this time of repentance
we call out for your mercy.
Bring us back to you
and to the life your Son won for us
by his death on the cross,
for he lives and reigns for ever and ever.

Daytime Prayer

HYMN, 47.

Midmorning

Ant.   The time of penance has come, the time to atone
for our sins and to seek our salvation.

READING   1 Thessalonians 4:1, 7

My brothers, we beg and exhort you in the Lord Jesus
that, even as you learned from us how to conduct yourselves in a way pleasing to God—which you are indeed
doing—so you must learn to make still greater progress.
God has not called us to immorality but to holiness.

Create a clean heart in me, O God.
— Renew in me a steadfast spirit.

Midday

Ant.   As I live, says the Lord, I do not wish the sinner
to die but to turn back to me and live.

READING   Isaiah 30:15, 18

Thus said the Lord God,
the Holy One of Israel:
By waiting and by calm you shall be saved,
in quiet and in trust your strength lies.
Yet the Lord is waiting to show you favor,
and he rises to pity you;
For the Lord is a God of justice:
blessed are all who wait for him!

Turn your face away from my sins.
— Blot out all my guilt.

Midafternoon

Ant.   Armed with God's justice and power, let us prove
ourselves through patient endurance.

READING   Deuteronomy 4:29-31

You shall seek the Lord, your God, and you shall indeed find him when you search after him with your whole heart and your whole soul. In your distress, when all these things shall have come upon you, you shall finally return to the Lord, your God, and heed his voice. Since the Lord, your God, is a merciful God, he will not abandon and destroy you, nor forget the covenant which under oath he made with your fathers.

My sacrifice to God is a contrite spirit.
__ A humble, contrite heart, O God, you will not spurn.

Prayer, as in Morning Prayer.

Evening Prayer II

HYMN, 33.

Ant. 1 Worship your Lord and God; serve him alone.

Psalms and canticle from Sunday, Week I, 1096.

Ant. 2 This is the time when you can win God's favor, the day when you can be saved.

Ant. 3 Now we must go up to Jerusalem where all that has been written about the Son of Man will be fulfilled.

READING   1 Corinthians 9:24-25

While all the runners in the stadium take part in the race, the award goes to one man. In that case, run so as to win! Athletes deny themselves all sorts of things. They do this to win a crown of leaves that withers, but we a crown that is imperishable.

RESPONSORY

Listen to us, O Lord, and have mercy, for we have sinned against you.

— Listen to us, O Lord, and have mercy, for we have sinned against you.

Christ Jesus, hear our humble petitions,
— for we have sinned against you.

Glory to the Father . . .
— Listen to us . . .

CANTICLE OF MARY

Ant.   Watch over us, eternal Savior; do not let the cunning tempter seize us. We place all our trust in your unfailing help.

INTERCESSIONS

All praise to God the Father who brought his chosen people to rebirth from imperishable seed through his eternal Word. Let us ask him as his children:

Lord, be gracious to your people.

God of mercy, hear the prayers we offer for all your people,
— may they hunger for your word more than for bodily food.

Give us a sincere and active love for our own nation and for all mankind,
— may we work always to build a world of peace and goodness.

Look with love on all to be reborn in baptism,
— that they may be living stones in your temple of the Spirit.

You moved Nineveh to repentance by the preaching of Jonah,
— in your mercy touch the hearts of sinners by the preaching of your word.

May the dying go in hope to meet Christ their judge,
— may they rejoice for ever in the vision of your glory.

Our Father . . .

Prayer

Father,
through our observance of Lent,
help us to understand the meaning
of your Son's death and resurrection,
and teach us to reflect it in our lives.

Grant this through our Lord Jesus Christ, your Son,
who lives and reigns with you and the Holy Spirit,
one God, for ever and ever.

Alternative Prayer

Lord our God,
you formed man from the clay of the earth
and breathed into him the spirit of life,
but he turned from your face and sinned.
In this time of repentance
we call out for your mercy.
Bring us back to you
and to the life your Son won for us
by his death on the cross,
for he lives and reigns for ever and ever.

MONDAY

Office of Readings

Turn away from sin and be faithful to the Gospel.
— The kingdom of God is at hand.

FIRST READING

From the book of Exodus   6:2-13

Another account of the call of Moses

God said to Moses, "I am the Lord. As God the Almighty I appeared to Abraham, Isaac and Jacob, but my name, Lord, I did not make known to them. I also established my covenant with them, to give them the land of Canaan, the land in which they were living as aliens. And now that I have heard the groaning of the Israelites, whom the Egyptians are treating as slaves, I am mindful of my covenant.

"Therefore, say to the Israelites: I am the Lord. I will free you from the forced labor of the Egyptians and will deliver you from their slavery. I will rescue you by my outstretched arm and with mighty acts of judgment. I will take you as my own people, and you shall have me as your God. You will know that I, the Lord, am your God when I free you from the labor of the Egyptians and bring you into the land which I swore to give to Abraham, Isaac and Jacob. I will give it to you as your own possession—I, the Lord!"

But when Moses told this to the Israelites, they would not listen to him because of their dejection and hard slavery.

Then the Lord said to Moses, "Go and tell Pharaoh, king of Egypt, to let the Israelites leave his land." But Moses protested to the Lord, "If the Israelites would not listen to me, how can it be that Pharaoh will listen to me, poor speaker that I am!" Still, the Lord, to bring the Israelites out of Egypt, spoke to Moses and Aaron and gave them his orders regarding both the Israelites and Pharaoh, king of Egypt.

RESPONSORY   See 1 Peter 2:9, 10; see Exodus 6:7, 6

You are a chosen race, a royal priesthood, a holy nation;
a people God has made his own.
Once you were not his people,
but now you are the people of God.
— I will adopt you as my own people,
and I will be your God.

I, your Lord, will free you from Egypt's slavery;
my mighty arm will bring you back.
— I will adopt you as my own people,
and I will be your God.

SECOND READING

From a sermon by Saint Gregory of Nazianzen, bishop
(Oratio 14, De pauperum amore, 23-25: PG 35, 887-890)

Let us show each other God's generosity

Recognize to whom you owe the fact that you exist, that you breathe, that you understand, that you are wise, and, above all, that you know God and hope for the kingdom of heaven and the vision of glory, now darkly and as in a mirror but then with greater fullness and purity. You have been made a son of God, coheir with Christ. Where did you get all this, and from whom?

Let me turn to what is of less importance: the visible world around us. What benefactor has enabled you to look out upon the beauty of the sky, the sun in its course, the circle of the moon, the countless number of stars, with the harmony and order that are theirs, like the music of a harp? Who has blessed you with rain, with the art of husbandry, with different kinds of food, with the arts, with houses, with laws, with states, with a life of humanity and culture, with friendship and the easy familiarity of kinship?

Who has given you dominion over animals, those that are tame and those that provide you with food? Who has made you lord and master of everything on earth? In short, who has endowed you with all that makes man superior to all other living creatures?

Is it not God who asks you now in your turn to show yourself generous above all other creatures and for the sake of all other creatures? Because we have received from him so many wonderful gifts, will we not be

ashamed to refuse him this one thing only, our generosity? Though he is God and Lord he is not afraid to be
known as our Father. Shall we for our part repudiate
those who are our kith and kin?

Brethren and friends, let us never allow ourselves to
misuse what has been given us by God's gift. If we do,
we shall hear Saint Peter say: *Be ashamed of yourselves
for holding on to what belongs to someone else. Resolve
to imitate God's justice, and no one will be poor.* Let us
not labor to heap up and hoard riches while others remain in need. If we do, the prophet Amos will speak out
against us with sharp and threatening words: *Come now,
you that say: When will the new moon be over, so that
we may start selling? When will sabbath be over, so that
we may start opening our treasures?*

Let us put into practice the supreme and primary law
of God. He sends down rain on just and sinful alike, and
causes the sun to rise on all without distinction. To all
earth's creatures he has given the broad earth, the
springs, the rivers and the forests. He has given the air
to the birds, and the waters to those who live in water.
He has given abundantly to all the basic needs of life, not
as a private possession, not restricted by law, not divided
by boundaries, but as common to all, amply and in rich
measure. His gifts are not deficient in any way, because
he wanted to give equality of blessing to equality of
worth, and to show the abundance of his generosity.

RESPONSORY   Luke 6:35; Matthew 5:45; Luke 6:36

Love your enemies, do good, share freely,
and ask for nothing in return.
Then you will be true sons of your Father,
— who makes his sun shine on the good and the bad,
and sends his rain upon honest and dishonest men alike.

Be compassionate as your Father is compassionate.
— who makes his sun shine on the good and the bad,
and sends his rain upon honest and dishonest men alike.

Prayer, as in Morning Prayer.

Morning Prayer

READING   Exodus 19:4-6a

You have seen for yourselves how I bore you up on
eagle wings and brought you here to myself. Therefore,
if you hearken to my voice and keep my covenant, you
shall be my special possession, dearer to me than all
other people, though all the earth is mine. You shall be
to me a kingdom of priests, a holy nation.

RESPONSORY

God himself will set me free, from the hunter's snare.
— God himself will set me free, from the hunter's snare.

From those who would trap me with lying words
— and from the hunter's snare.

Glory to the Father . . .
— God himself will . . .

CANTICLE OF ZECHARIAH

Ant.   You have been blessed by my Father; come and
receive the kingdom prepared for you from the
foundation of the world.

INTERCESSIONS

Praise to Jesus, our Savior; by his death he has opened
for us the way of salvation. Let us ask him:
  Lord, guide your people to walk in your ways.
God of mercy, you gave us new life through baptism,
— make us grow day by day in your likeness.

May our generosity today bring joy to those in need,
— in helping them may we find you.
Help us to do what is good, right and true in your sight,
— and to seek you always with undivided hearts.
Forgive our sins against the unity of your family,
— make us one in heart and spirit.

Our Father . . .

Prayer

God our savior,
bring us back to you
and fill our minds with your wisdom.
May we be enriched by our observance of Lent.

Grant this through our Lord Jesus Christ, your Son,
who lives and reigns with you and the Holy Spirit,
one God, for ever and ever.

Daytime Prayer

Midmorning

Ant.   The time of penance has come, the time to atone
for our sins and to seek our salvation.

READING   Wisdom 11:23:24a

You have mercy on all, O Lord, because you can do all
things;
and you overlook the sins of men that they may
repent.
For you love all things that are
and loathe nothing that you have made.

Create a clean heart in me, O God.
— Renew in me a steadfast spirit.

Midday

Ant.   As I live, says the Lord, I do not wish the sinner
to die but to turn back to me and live.

READING   Ezekiel 18:23

Do I indeed derive any pleasure from the death of the
wicked? says the Lord God. Do I not rather rejoice
when he turns from his evil way that he may live?

Turn your face away from my sins.
— Blot out all my guilt.

Midafternoon

Ant.   Armed with God's justice and power, let us prove
        ourselves through patient endurance.

READING   Isaiah 58:7

Share your bread with the hungry,
    shelter the oppressed and the homeless;
Clothe the naked when you see them,
    and do not turn your back on your own.

My sacrifice to God is a contrite spirit.
— A humble, contrite heart, O God, you will not spurn.

Prayer, as in Morning Prayer.

Evening Prayer

READING   Romans 12:1-2

Brothers, I beg you through the mercy of God to offer
your bodies as a living sacrifice holy and acceptable to
God, your spiritual worship. Do not conform yourselves
to this age but be transformed by the renewal of your
mind, so that you may judge what is God's will, what is
good, pleasing and perfect.

RESPONSORY

To you, O Lord, I make my prayer for mercy.
— To you, O Lord, I make my prayer for mercy.

Heal my soul, for I have sinned against you.
— I make my prayer for mercy.

Glory to the Father . . .
__ To you, O Lord . . .

CANTICLE OF MARY

Ant.   Whatever you do for the least of my brothers, you do for me.

INTERCESSIONS

Our Lord Jesus Christ has saved us from our sins. As his people, let us call out to him:
   Jesus, Son of David, have mercy on us.

Lord Christ, we pray for your holy Church; you gave yourself up to make it holy, cleansing it with water and the life-giving word,
__ renew it constantly, and purify it by penance.

Good Master, show young people the way you have chosen for each of them,
__ may they walk in it, and find fulfillment.

In your compassion you healed all forms of sickness; bring hope to the sick and raise them up,
__ teach us to love and care for them.

Make us mindful of the dignity you gave us in baptism,
__ may we live for you at every moment.

May the dead rise to glory in your peace,
__ grant us with them a share in your kingdom.

Our Father . . .

Prayer

God our savior,
bring us back to you
and fill our minds with your wisdom.
May we be enriched by our observance of Lent.
Grant this through our Lord Jesus Christ, your Son,
who lives and reigns with you and the Holy Spirit,
one God, for ever and ever.

TUESDAY

Office of Readings

This is the favorable time.
— This is the day of salvation.

First Reading

From the book of Exodus　　　　　　6:29—7:25

The first plague sent upon Egypt

The Lord spoke to Moses, saying, "I am the Lord. Repeat to Pharaoh, king of Egypt, all that I tell you." But Moses protested to the Lord, "Since I am a poor speaker, how can it be that Pharaoh will listen to me?"

The Lord answered him, "See! I have made you as God to Pharaoh, and Aaron your brother shall act as your prophet. You shall tell him all that I command you. In turn, your brother Aaron shall tell Pharaoh to let the Israelites leave his land. Yet I will make Pharaoh so obstinate that, despite the many signs and wonders that I will work in the land of Egypt, he will not listen to you. Therefore I will lay my hand on Egypt and by great acts of judgment I will bring the hosts of my people, the Israelites, out of the land of Egypt, so that the Egyptians may learn that I am the Lord, as I stretch out my hand against Egypt and lead the Israelites out of their midst."

Moses and Aaron did as the Lord had commanded them. Moses was eighty years old and Aaron eighty-three when they spoke to Pharaoh.

The Lord told Moses and Aaron, "If Pharaoh demands that you work a sign or wonder, you shall say to Aaron: Take your staff and throw it down before Pharaoh, and it will be changed into a snake." Then Moses and Aaron went to Pharaoh and did as the Lord had commanded. Aaron threw his staff down before Pharaoh and his servants, and it was changed into a snake.

Pharaoh, in turn, summoned wise men and sorcerers, and they also, the magicians of Egypt, did likewise by their magic arts. Each one threw down his staff, and it was changed into a snake. But Aaron's staff swallowed their staffs. Pharaoh, however, was obstinate and would not listen to them, just as the Lord had foretold.

Then the Lord said to Moses, "Pharaoh is obdurate in refusing to let the people go. Tomorrow morning, when he sets out for the water, go and present yourself by the river bank, holding in your hand the staff that turned into a serpent. Say to him: The Lord, the God of the Hebrews, sent me to you with the message: Let my people go to worship me in the desert. But as yet you have not listened. The Lord now says: This is how you shall know that I am the Lord. I will strike the water of the river with the staff I hold, and it shall be changed into blood. The fish in the river shall die, and the river itself shall become so polluted that the Egyptians will be unable to drink its water."

The Lord then said to Moses, "Say to Aaron: Take your staff and stretch out your hand over the waters of Egypt—their streams and canals and pools, all their supplies of water—that they may become blood. Throughout the land of Egypt there shall be blood, even in the wooden pails and stone jars."

Moses and Aaron did as the Lord had commanded. Aaron raised his staff and struck the waters of the river in full view of Pharaoh and his servants, and all the water of the river was changed into blood. The fish in the river died, and the river itself became so polluted that the Egyptians could not drink its water. There was blood throughout the land of Egypt.

But the Egyptian magicians did the same by their magic arts. So Pharaoh remained obstinate and would not listen to Moses and Aaron, just as the Lord had foretold. He turned away and went into his house, with no concern even for this. All the Egyptians had to dig in the neighborhood of the river for drinking water, since they could not drink the river water. Seven days passed after the Lord had struck the river.

RESPONSORY   Revelation 16:4-5, 6, 7

The angel poured out the phial into the river,
and the waters turned into blood.
Then I heard him cry:
You are just, O Holy One,
and just is the punishment you have decreed.
— These men have spilled the blood of the saints and
   the prophets.

Then I heard another angel cry from the altar:
Lord God Almighty, your judgments are true and just.
— These men have . . .

SECOND READING

From a treatise on the Lord's Prayer by Saint Cyprian, bishop and martyr

(Cap. 1-3: CSEL 3, 267-268)

He has given us life; he has also taught us how to pray

Dear brothers, the commands of the Gospel are nothing else than God's lessons, the foundations on which to build up hope, the supports for strengthening faith, the food that nourishes the heart. They are the rudder for keeping us on the right course, the protection that keeps our salvation secure. As they instruct the receptive minds of believers on earth, they lead safely to the kingdom of heaven.

God willed that many things should be said by the prophets, his servants, and listened to by his people. How much greater are the things spoken by the Son. These are now witnessed to by the very Word of God who spoke through the prophets. The Word of God does not now command us to prepare the way for his coming: he comes in person and opens up the way for us and directs us toward it. Before, we wandered in the darkness of death, aimlessly and blindly. Now we are enlightened by the light of grace, and are to keep to the highway of life, with the Lord to precede and direct us.

The Lord has given us many counsels and commandments to help us toward salvation. He has even given us a pattern of prayer, instructing us on how we are to pray. He has given us life, and with his accustomed generosity, he has also taught us how to pray. He has made it easy for us to be heard as we pray to the Father in the words taught us by the Son.

He had already foretold that the hour was coming when true worshipers would worship the Father in spirit and in truth. He fulfilled what he had promised before, so that we who have received the spirit and the truth through the holiness he has given us may worship in truth and in the spirit through the prayer he has taught.

What prayer could be more a prayer in the spirit than the one given us by Christ, by whom the Holy Spirit was sent upon us? What prayer could be more a prayer in the truth than the one spoken by the lips of the Son, who is truth himself? It follows that to pray in any other way than the Son has taught us is not only the result of ignorance but of sin. He himself has commanded it, and has said: *You reject the command of God, to set up your own tradition.*

So, my brothers, let us pray as God our master has taught us. To ask the Father in words his Son has given us, to let him hear the prayer of Christ ringing in his ears, is to make our prayer one of friendship, a family prayer. Let the Father recognize the words of his Son. Let the Son who lives in our hearts be also on our lips. We have him as an advocate for sinners before the Father; when we ask forgiveness for our sins, let us use the words given by our advocate. He tells us: *Whatever you ask the Father in my name, he will give you.* What more effective prayer could we then make in the name of Christ than in the words of his own prayer?

RESPONSORY   John 16:24; 14:13

Until now you have asked for nothing in my name,
— ask and you will receive that your joy may be full.

Whatever you ask the Father in my name I will give you, that the Father may be glorified in the Son.
— Ask and you . . .

Prayer, as in Morning Prayer.

Morning Prayer

READING   Joel 2:12-13

Return to me with your whole heart,
    with fasting, and weeping, and mourning;
Rend your hearts, not your garments,
    and return to the Lord, your God.
For gracious and merciful is he,
    slow to anger, rich in kindness,
    and relenting in punishment.

RESPONSORY

God himself will set me free, from the hunter's snare.
— God himself will set me free, from the hunter's snare.

From those who would trap me with lying words
— and from the hunter's snare.

Glory to the Father . . .
— God himself will . . .

CANTICLE OF ZECHARIAH

Ant. Lord, teach us to pray as John taught his
disciples.

INTERCESSIONS

Praise to Christ, who has given us himself as the bread
from heaven. Let us pray to him, saying:
*Jesus, you feed and heal our souls; come to strengthen
us.*
Lord, feed us at the banquet of the eucharist,
— with all the gifts of your paschal sacrifice.
Give us a perfect heart to receive your word,
— that we may bring forth fruit in patience.
Make us eager to work with you in building a better
world,
— so that it may listen to your Church and its gospel of
peace.
We confess, Lord, that we have sinned,
— wash us clean by your gift of salvation.

Our Father . . .

Prayer

Father,
look on us, your children.

Midafternoon

Ant. Armed with God's justice and power, let us prove
ourselves through patient endurance.

READING   Isaiah 58:1-2

Cry out full-throated and unsparingly,
 lift up your voice like a trumpet blast;
Tell my people their wickedness,
 and the house of Jacob their sins.
They seek me day after day,
 and desire to know my ways,
Like a nation that has done what is just
 and not abandoned the law of their God.

My sacrifice to God is a contrite spirit.
—A humble, contrite heart, O God, you will not spurn.

Prayer, as in Morning Prayer.

Evening Prayer

READING   James 2:14, 17, 18b

My brothers, what good is it to profess faith without
practicing it? Such faith has no power to save one, has
it? So it is with the faith that does nothing in practice.
It is thoroughly lifeless. Show me faith without works,
and I will show you the faith that underlies my works!

RESPONSORY

To you, O Lord, I make my prayer for mercy.
—To you, O Lord, I make my prayer for mercy.

Heal my soul, for I have sinned against you.
—I make my prayer for mercy.

Glory to the Father . . .
— To you, O Lord, I make my prayer for mercy.

CANTICLE OF MARY

Ant.   When you wish to pray, go to your room, shut the door, and pray to your Father in secret.

INTERCESSIONS

Christ our Lord has warned us to watch and pray to avoid temptation. With our whole heart let us pray to him:

Turn to us, Lord, and have mercy.

Jesus, our Christ, you promised to be with those who pray in your name,
— help us always to pray with you to the Father in the Holy Spirit.

Bridegroom of the Church, cleanse her from every stain,
— teach her to walk in hope and in the power of the Holy Spirit.

Friend of the human race, teach us concern for our neighbor as you have commanded,
— that all may see you more clearly as the light of the world.

King of peace, give your peace to the world,
— that your presence may reveal your saving power in every place.

Open the door of eternal happiness to all the dead,
— welcome them into the glory of unending life.

Our Father . . .

Prayer

Father,
look on us, your children.
Through the discipline of Lent
help us to grow in our desire for you.

We ask this through our Lord Jesus Christ, your Son,
who lives and reigns with you and the Holy Spirit,
one God, for ever and ever.

WEDNESDAY

Office of Readings

Turn back to the Lord and do penance.
— Be renewed in heart and spirit.

FIRST READING

From the book of Exodus   10:21—11:10

*The plague of darkness and the warning of the plague
to be visited upon the firstborn*

The Lord said to Moses, "Stretch out your hand
toward the sky, that over the land of Egypt there may be
such intense darkness that one can feel it." So Moses
stretched out his hand toward the sky, and there was
dense darkness throughout the land of Egypt for three
days. Men could not see one another, nor could they
move from where they were, for three days. But all the
Israelites had light where they dwelt.

Pharaoh then summoned Moses and Aaron and said,
"Go and worship the Lord. Your little ones, too, may
go with you. But your flocks and herds must remain."
Moses replied, "You must also grant us sacrifices and
holocausts to offer up to the Lord, our God. Hence, our
livestock also must go with us. Not an animal must be
left behind. Some of them we must sacrifice to the Lord,
our God, but we ourselves shall not know which ones we
must sacrifice to him until we arrive at the place itself."

But the Lord made Pharaoh obstinate, and he would not let them go. "Leave my presence," Pharaoh said to him, "and see to it that you do not appear before me again! The day you appear before me you shall die!" Moses replied, "Well said! I will never appear before you again."

Then the Lord told Moses, "One more plague will I bring upon Pharaoh and upon Egypt. After that he will let you depart. In fact, he will not merely let you go; he will drive you away. Instruct your people that every man is to ask his neighbor, and every woman her neighbor, for silver and gold articles and for clothing." The Lord indeed made the Egyptians well-disposed toward the people; Moses himself was very highly regarded by Pharaoh's servants and the people in the land of Egypt.

Moses then said, "Thus says the Lord: At midnight I will go forth through Egypt. Every first-born in this land shall die, from the first-born of Pharaoh on the throne to the first-born of the slave-girl at the handmill, as well as all the first-born of the animals. Then there shall be loud wailing throughout the land of Egypt, such as has never been, nor will ever be again. But among the Israelites and their animals not even a dog shall growl, so that you may know how the Lord distinguishes between the Egyptians and the Israelites. All these servants of yours shall then come down to me, and prostrate before me, they shall beg me, 'Leave us, you and all your followers!' Only then will I depart." With that he left Pharaoh's presence in hot anger.

The Lord said to Moses, "Pharaoh refuses to listen to you that my wonders may be multiplied in the land of Egypt." Thus, although Moses and Aaron performed these various wonders in Pharaoh's presence, the Lord made Pharaoh obstinate, and he would not let the Israelites leave his land.

RESPONSORY   Wisdom 18:4; 17:20; 18:1

How well those who enslaved your children
deserved to be deprived of light,
— for through your children
the imperishable light of the law
was to be given to the world.

On Egypt the deep gloom of night descended,
but a radiant light shone for your holy ones.
— For through your . . . .

SECOND READING

From a demonstration by Aphraates, bishop

(Dem. 11, De circumcisione, 11-12: PS 1, 498-503)

Circumcision of the heart

Law and covenant have been entirely changed. God changed the first pact with Adam, and gave a new one to Noah. He gave another to Abraham, and changed this to give a new one to Moses. When the covenant with Moses was no longer observed, he gave another pact in this last age, a pact never again to be changed.

He established a law for Adam, that he could not eat of the tree of life. He gave to Noah the sign of the rainbow in the clouds. He then gave Abraham, chosen for his faith, the mark and seal of circumcision for his descendants. Moses was given the Passover lamb, the propitiation for the people.

All these covenants were different from each other. Moreover, the circumcision that is approved by the giver of those covenants is the kind spoken of by Jeremiah:

Circumcise your hearts. If God's pact with Abraham was firm, so also is this covenant firm and trustworthy, nor can any other law be laid down, whether it originates outside the law or among those subject to the law.

God gave Moses a law together with his prescriptions and precepts, and when it was no longer kept, he made the law and its precepts of no avail. He promised a new covenant, different from the first, though the giver of both is one and the same. This is the covenant that he promised: *All shall know me from the least to the greatest.* In this covenant there is no longer any circumcision of the flesh, any seal upon the people.

We know, dearly beloved, that God established different laws in different generations which were in force as long as it pleased him. Afterward they were made obsolete. In the words of the Apostle: *In former times the kingdom of God existed in each generation under different signs.*

Moreover, our God is truthful and his commandments are most trustworthy. Every covenant was proved firm and trustworthy in its own time, and those who have been circumcised in heart are brought to life and receive a second circumcision beside the true Jordan, the waters of baptism that bring forgiveness of sins.

Jesus, son of Nun, renewed the people's circumcision with a knife of stone when he had crossed the Jordan with the Israelites. Jesus, our Savior, renews the circumcision of the heart for the nations who have believed in him and are washed by baptism: circumcision by *the sword of his word, sharper than a two-edged sword.*

Jesus, son of Nun, led the people across the Jordan into the promised land. Jesus, our Savior, has promised the land of the living to all who have crossed the true Jordan, and have believed and are circumcised in heart.

Blessed, then, are those who are circumcised in heart, and have been reborn in water through the second circumcision. They will receive their inheritance with Abraham, the faithful leader and father of all nations, for his faith was credited to him for righteousness.

RESPONSORY   Hebrews 8:8, 10; 2 Corinthians 3:3

I will make a new covenant with the house of Israel.
I will put my laws in their minds
— and inscribe them on their hearts,
not with ink but with the spirit of the living God.

I will not write my law upon tablets of stone,
but upon the tablets of human hearts.
— And inscribe them . . .

Prayer, as in Morning Prayer.

Morning Prayer

READING   Deuteronomy 7:6, 8-9

The Lord, your God, has chosen you from all the nations on the face of the earth to be a people peculiarly his own. It was because the Lord loved you and because of his fidelity to the oath he had sworn to your fathers, that he brought you out with his strong hand from the place of slavery, and ransomed you from the hand of Pharaoh, king of Egypt. Understand, then, that the Lord, your God, is God indeed, the faithful God who keeps his merciful covenant to the thousandth generation toward those who love him and keep his commandments.

RESPONSORY

God himself will set me free, from the hunter's snare.
— God himself will set me free, from the hunter's snare.

From those who would trap me with lying words
— and from the hunter's snare.

Glory to the Father . . .
— God himself will . . .

CANTICLE OF ZECHARIAH

Ant.   This evil and faithless generation asks for a sign,
       but no sign will be given it except the sign of the
       prophet Jonah.

INTERCESSIONS

Blessed be God, the giver of salvation, who decreed that
    mankind should become a new creation in himself,
    when all would be made new. With great confidence
    let us ask him:
    Lord, renew us in your Spirit.
Lord, you promised a new heaven and a new earth; re-
    new us daily through your Spirit,
— that we may enjoy your presence for ever in the
    heavenly Jerusalem.
Help us to work with you to make this world alive with
    your Spirit,
— and to build on earth a city of justice, love and peace.
Free us from all negligence and sloth,
— and give us joy in your gifts of grace.
Deliver us from evil,
— and from slavery to the senses, which blinds us to
    goodness.

Our Father . . .

Prayer

Lord,
look upon us and hear our prayer.
By the good works you inspire,
help us to discipline our bodies
and to be renewed in spirit.

Grant this through our Lord Jesus Christ, your Son,
who lives and reigns with you and the Holy Spirit,
one God, for ever and ever.

Daytime Prayer

Midmorning

Ant. The time of penance has come, the time to atone
for our sins and to seek our salvation.

READING   Ezekiel 18:30b-32

Turn and be converted from all your crimes, that
they may be no cause of guilt for you. Cast away from
you all the crimes you have committed, and make for
yourselves a new heart and a new spirit. Why should
you die, O house of Israel? For I have no pleasure in
the death of anyone who dies, says the Lord God. Return and live!

Create a clean heart in me, O God.
— Renew in me a steadfast spirit.

Midday

Ant. As I live, says the Lord, I do not wish the sinner
to die but to turn back to me and live.

READING   Zechariah 1:3b-4b

Return to me, says the Lord of hosts, and I will return
to you. Be not like your fathers whom the former pro

phets warned: Turn from your evil ways and from your
wicked deeds.

Turn your face away from my sins.
— Blot out all my guilt.

Midafternoon

Ant.   Armed with God's justice and power, let us prove
        ourselves through patient endurance.

READING   Daniel 4:24b

Atone for your sins by good deeds, and for your misdeeds by kindness to the poor; then your prosperity will
be long.

My sacrifice to God is a contrite spirit.
— A humble, contrite heart, O God, you will not spurn.

Prayer, as in Morning Prayer.

Evening Prayer

READING   Philippians 2:12b-15a

Work with anxious concern to achieve your salvation.
It is God who, in his good will toward you, begets in
you any measure of desire or achievement. In everything
you do, act without grumbling or arguing; prove yourselves innocent and straightforward, children of God
without reproach.

RESPONSORY

To you, O Lord, I make my prayer for mercy.
— To you, O Lord, I make my prayer for mercy.

Heal my soul, for I have sinned against you.
— I make my prayer for mercy.

Glory to the Father . . .
— To you, O Lord . . .

CANTICLE OF MARY

Ant. As Jonah was three days and three nights in the
belly of the whale, so will the Son of Man spend
three days and three nights in the heart of the
earth.

INTERCESSIONS

Blessed be almighty God, who watches over us as a
Father; he knows all our needs but wants us to seek
first his kingdom. Let us cry out to him as his people:
May your kingdom come, that justice may reign.

Father of all holiness, you gave us Christ as the shepherd
of our souls; stay with your shepherds and the flock
entrusted to them, do not leave this flock without the
loving care of its shepherd,
— do not leave your shepherds without an obedient
flock to follow them.

Teach Christians to help the weak with loving care,
— and in serving them to serve your Son.

Gather into your Church those who do not yet believe,
— and help them to build it up by good deeds done for
love of you.

Help us to turn to you for forgiveness,
— and, as you forgive us, reconcile us also with your
Church.

May the dead pass from this world to eternal life,
— to be with you for ever.

Our Father . . .

Prayer

Lord,
look upon us and hear our prayer.

By the good works you inspire,
help us to discipline our bodies
and to be renewed in spirit.

Grant this through our Lord Jesus Christ, your Son,
who lives and reigns with you and the Holy Spirit,
one God, for ever and ever.

THURSDAY

Office of Readings

Whoever meditates on the law of the Lord.
—Will bring forth much fruit at harvest time.

FIRST READING

From the book of Exodus　　　　　12:1-20

The Passover and unleavened bread

The Lord said to Moses and Aaron in the land of
Egypt, "This month shall stand at the head of your cal-
endar; you shall reckon it the first month of the year.
Tell the whole community of Israel:

"On the tenth of this month every one of your families
must procure for itself a lamb, one apiece for each household. If a family is too small for a whole lamb, it shall
join the nearest household in procuring one and shall
share in the lamb in proportion to the number of per-
sons who partake of it. The lamb must be a year-old
male and without blemish. You may take it from either
the sheep or the goats. You shall keep it until the fourteenth day of this month, and then, with the whole assembly of Israel present, it shall be slaughtered during
the evening twilight. They shall take some of its blood

and apply it to the two doorposts and the lintel of every house in which they partake of the lamb. That same night they shall eat its roasted flesh with unleavened bread and bitter herbs. It shall not be eaten raw or boiled, but roasted whole, with its head and shanks and inner organs. None of it must be kept beyond the next morning; whatever is left over in the morning shall be burned up.

"This is how you are to eat it: with your loins girt, sandals on your feet and your staff in hand, you shall eat like those who are in flight. It is the Passover of the Lord.

"For on this same night I will go through Egypt, striking down every first-born of the land, both man and beast, and executing judgment on all the gods of Egypt —I, the Lord! But the blood will mark the houses where you are. Seeing the blood, I will pass over you; thus, when I strike the land of Egypt, no destructive blow will come upon you.

"This day shall be a memorial feast for you, which all your generations shall celebrate with pilgrimage to the Lord, as a perpetual institution. For seven days you must eat unleavened bread. From the very first day you shall have your houses clear of all leaven. Whoever eats leavened bread from the first day to the seventh shall be cut off from Israel. On the first day you shall hold a sacred assembly, and likewise on the seventh. On these days you shall not do any sort of work, except to prepare the food that everyone needs.

"Keep, then, this custom of the unleavened bread. Since it was on this very day that I brought your ranks out of the land of Egypt, you must celebrate this day throughout your generations as a perpetual institution. From the evening of the fourteenth day of the first month until the evening of the twenty-first day of this month you shall eat unleavened bread. For seven days no leaven may be found in your houses. Anyone, be he a resident alien or a native, who eats leavened food shall be cut off from the community of Israel. Nothing leavened may you eat; wherever you dwell you may eat only unleavened bread."

RESPONSORY   Revelation 5:8, 9; see 1 Peter 1:18, 19

The elders fell prostrate before the Lamb
and sang this new song:
— By your blood, O Lord, you have ransomed us for
  God.

We have been redeemed not by perishable goods like
  gold and silver
but by the precious blood of Christ,
the lamb without spot or blemish.
— By your blood . . .

SECOND READING

From a homily by Saint Asterius of Amasea, bishop

(Hom. 13: PG 40, 355-358. 362)

Be shepherds like the Lord

You were made in the image of God. If then you wish to resemble him, follow his example. Since the very name you bear as Christians is a profession of love for men, imitate the love of Christ.

Reflect for a moment on the wealth of his kindness. Before he came as a man to be among men, he sent John the Baptist to preach repentance and lead men to practice it. John himself was preceded by the prophets, who were to teach the people to repent, to return to God and to amend their lives. Then Christ came himself, and with his own lips cried out: *Come to me, all you who labor and are overburdened, and I will give you rest.* How did he receive those who listened to his call? He readily forgave them their sins; he freed them instantly from all that troubled them. The Word made them holy; the Spirit set his seal on them. The old Adam was buried in the waters of baptism; the new man was reborn to the vigor of grace.

What was the result? Those who had been God's enemies became his friends, those estranged from him became his sons, those who did not know him came to worship and love him.

Let us then be shepherds like the Lord. We must meditate on the Gospel, and as we see in this mirror the example of zeal and loving kindness, we should become thoroughly schooled in these virtues.

For there, obscurely, in the form of a parable, we see a shepherd who had a hundred sheep. When one of them was separated from the flock and lost its way, that shepherd did not remain with the sheep who kept together at pasture. No, he went off to look for the stray. He crossed many valleys and thickets, he climbed great and towering mountains, he spent much time and labor in wandering through solitary places until at last he found his sheep.

When he found it, he did not chastise it; he did not use rough blows to drive it back, but gently placed it on his own shoulders and carried it back to the flock. He took greater joy in this one sheep, lost and found, than in all the others.

Let us look more closely at the hidden meaning of this parable. The sheep is more than a sheep, the shepherd more than a shepherd. They are examples enshrining holy truths. They teach us that we should not look on men as lost or beyond hope; we should not abandon them when they are in danger or be slow to come to their help. When they turn away from the right path and wander, we must lead them back, and rejoice at their return, welcoming them back into the company of those who lead good and holy lives.

RESPONSORY   Zechariah 7:9; Matthew 6:14

Judge with true judgment,
— and let each one be merciful and forgiving to his brother.

If you forgive the sins of others,
your Father in heaven will also forgive your sins.
— And let each . . .

Prayer, as in Morning Prayer.

Morning Prayer

READING   See 1 Kings 8:51-53a

We are your people and your inheritance. Thus may your eyes be open to the petition of your servant and to the petition of your people Israel. Hear us whenever we call upon you, because you have set us apart among all the peoples of the earth of your inheritance.

RESPONSORY

God himself will set me free, from the hunter's snare.
— God himself will set me free, from the hunter's snare.

From those who would trap me with lying words
— and from the hunter's snare.

Glory to the Father . . .
— God himself will . . .

CANTICLE OF ZECHARIAH

Ant.   If you, evil as you are, know how to give your
       children what is good, how much more will your
       Father in heaven pour out his gifts on all who
       pray to him.

INTERCESSIONS

Christ our Lord came among us as the light of the world,
    that we might walk in his light, and not in the dark-
    ness of death. Let us praise him and cry out to him:
    Let your word be a lamp to guide us.
God of mercy, help us today to grow in your likeness,
— that we who sinned in Adam may rise again in Christ.
Let your word be a lamp to guide us,
— that we may live the truth and grow always in your
    love.
Teach us to be faithful in seeking the common good for
    your sake,
— that your light may shine on the whole human family
    by means of your Church.
Touch our hearts to seek your friendship more and more,
— and to make amends for our sins against your wisdom
    and goodness.

Our Father . . .

Prayer

Father,
without you we can do nothing.
By your Spirit help us to know what is right
and to be eager in doing your will.

We ask this through our Lord Jesus Christ, your Son,
who lives and reigns with you and the Holy Spirit,
one God, for ever and ever.

Daytime Prayer

Midmorning

Ant.   The time of penance has come, the time to atone
for our sins and to seek our salvation.

READING   Isaiah 55:6-7

Seek the Lord while he may be found,
   call him while he is near.
Let the scoundrel forsake his way,
   and the wicked man his thoughts;
Let him turn to the Lord for mercy;
   to our God, who is generous in forgiving.

Create a clean heart in me, O God.
— Renew in me a steadfast spirit.

Midday

Ant.   As I live, says the Lord, I do not wish the sinner
to die but to turn back to me and live.

READING   Deuteronomy 30:2-3a

Provided that you and your children return to the
Lord, your God, and heed his voice with all your heart
and all your soul, just as I now command you, the Lord,
your God, will change your lot and take pity on you.

Turn your face away from my sins.
— Blot out all my guilt.

Midafternoon

Ant.   Armed with God's justice and power, let us prove
       ourselves through patient endurance.

READING   Hebrews 10:35-36

Do not surrender your confidence; it will have great
reward. You need patience to do God's will and receive
what he has promised.

My sacrifice to God is a contrite spirit.
— A humble, contrite heart, O God, you will not spurn.

Prayer, as in Morning Prayer.

Evening Prayer

READING   James 4:7-8, 10

Submit to God; resist the devil and he will take flight.
Draw close to God, and he will draw close to you.
Cleanse your hands, you sinners; purify your hearts, you
backsliders. Be humbled in the sight of the Lord and he
will raise you on high.

RESPONSORY

To you, O Lord, I make my prayer for mercy.
— To you, O Lord, I make my prayer for mercy.

Heal my soul, for I have sinned against you.
— I make my prayer for mercy.

Glory to the Father . . .
— To you, O Lord . . .

CANTICLE OF MARY

Ant.   Ask and you shall receive, seek and you shall find,
       knock and the door shall be opened to you.

INTERCESSIONS

Christ the Lord gave us a new commandment, of love
for each other. Let us pray to him:
Lord, build up your people in love.
Good Master, teach us to love you in our neighbor,
— and in serving them to serve you.
On the cross you asked pardon for your executioners,
— give us strength to love our enemies and pray for
those who persecute us.
Through the mystery of your body and blood, deepen
our love, our perseverance and our trust,
— strengthen the weak, console the sorrowful, and give
hope to the dying.
Light of the world, you gave light to the man born blind
when he had washed in the pool of Siloam,
— enlighten catechumens through the water of baptism
and the word of life.
Give to the dead the perfect joy of your eternal love,
— and number us also among your chosen ones.

Our Father . . .

Prayer

Father,
without you we can do nothing.
By your Spirit help us to know what is right
and to be eager in doing your will.

We ask this through our Lord Jesus Christ, your Son,
who lives and reigns with you and the Holy Spirit,
one God, for ever and ever.

FRIDAY

Office of Readings

Turn back to the Lord your God.
— He is kind and merciful.

First Reading

From the book of Exodus   12:21-36

The plague inflicted on the firstborn

Moses called all the elders of Israel and said to them, "Go and procure lambs for your families, and slaughter them as Passover victims. Then take a bunch of hyssop, and dipping it in the blood that is in the basin, sprinkle the lintel and the two doorposts with this blood. But none of you shall go outdoors until morning. For the Lord will go by, striking down the Egyptians. Seeing the blood on the lintel and the two doorposts, the Lord will pass over that door and not let the destroyer come into your houses to strike you down.

"You shall observe this as a perpetual ordinance for yourselves and your descendants. Thus, you must also observe this rite when you have entered the land which the Lord will give you as he promised. When your children ask you, 'What does this rite of yours mean?' you shall reply, 'This is the Passover sacrifice of the Lord, who passed over the houses of the Israelites in Egypt; when he struck down the Egyptians, he spared our houses.' "

Then the people bowed down in worship, and the Israelites went and did as the Lord had commanded Moses and Aaron.

At midnight the Lord slew every first-born in the land of Egypt, from the first-born of Pharaoh on the throne to the first-born of the prisoner in the dungeon, as well as all the first-born of the animals. Pharaoh arose in the night, he and all his servants and all the Egyptians; and there was loud wailing throughout Egypt, for there was not a house without its dead.

During the night Pharaoh summoned Moses and Aaron and said, "Leave my people at once, you and the Israelites with you! Go and worship the Lord as you said. Take your flocks, too, and your herds, as you demanded, and begone; and you will be doing me a favor."

The Egyptians likewise urged the people on, to hasten their departure from the land; they thought that otherwise they would all die. The people, therefore, took their dough before it was leavened, in their kneading bowls wrapped in their cloaks on their shoulders. The Israelites did as Moses had commanded: they asked the Egyptians for articles of silver and gold and for clothing. The Lord indeed had made the Egyptians so well-disposed toward the people that they let them have whatever they asked for. Thus did they despoil the Egyptians.

RESPONSORY   Exodus 12:7, 13; 1 Peter 1:18, 19

The children of Israel shall put the blood of the lamb
on the doorposts and lintels of their houses.
— This blood will be a sign to you.

You have been redeemed by the precious blood of
   Christ,
the lamb without blemish.
— This blood will . . .

SECOND READING

From the Mirror of Love by Saint Aelred, abbot

(Lib. 3, 5: PL 195, 582)

Christ, the model of brotherly love

The perfection of brotherly love lies in the love of one's enemies. We can find no greater inspiration for this than grateful remembrance of the wonderful patience of Christ. He who is *more fair than all the sons of men* offered his fair face to be spat upon by sinful men; he allowed those eyes that rule the universe to be blindfolded by wicked men; he bared his back to the scourges; he submitted that head which strikes terror in principalities and powers to the sharpness of the thorns; he gave himself up to be mocked and reviled, and at the end endured the cross, the nails, the lance, the gall, the vinegar, remaining always gentle, meek and full of peace.

In short, *he was led like a sheep to the slaughter, and like a lamb before the shearers he kept silent, and did not open his mouth.*

Who could listen to that wonderful prayer, so full of warmth, of love, of unshakable serenity—*Father, forgive them*—and hesitate to embrace his enemies with overflowing love? *Father,* he says, *forgive them.* Is any gentleness, any love, lacking in this prayer?

Yet he put into it something more. It was not enough to pray for them: he wanted also to make excuses for them. *Father, forgive them, for they do not know what they are doing.* They are great sinners, yes, but they have little judgment; therefore, *Father, forgive them.* They are nailing me to the cross, but they do not know who it is that they are nailing to the cross: *if they had known, they would never have crucified the Lord of glory;* therefore, *Father, forgive them.* They think it is a lawbreaker, an impostor claiming to be God, a seducer of the people. I have hidden my face from them, and they do not recognize my glory; therefore, *Father, forgive them, for they do not know what they are doing.*

If someone wishes to love himself he must not allow himself to be corrupted by indulging his sinful nature. If he wishes to resist the promptings of his sinful nature he must enlarge the whole horizon of his love to contemplate the loving gentleness of the humanity of the Lord. Further, if he wishes to savor the joy of brotherly love with greater perfection and delight, he must extend even to his enemies the embrace of true love.

But if he wishes to prevent this fire of divine love from growing cold because of injuries received, let him keep the eyes of his soul always fixed on the serene patience of his beloved Lord and Savior.

RESPONSORY   Isaiah 53:12; Luke 23:34

He surrendered himself to death
and was counted among the wicked.
— He bore the crimes of many
and prayed all the while for sinners.

Jesus prayed: Father, forgive them;
they do not know what they are doing.
— He bore the . . .

Prayer, as in Morning Prayer.

Morning Prayer

READING   Isaiah 53:11b-12

Through his suffering, my servant shall justify many,
    and their guilt he shall bear.
Therefore I will give him his portion among the great,
    and he shall divide the spoils with the mighty,
Because he surrendered himself to death
    and was counted among the wicked;
And he shall take away the sins of many
    and win pardon for their offenses.

RESPONSORY

God himself will set me free, from the hunter's snare.
— God himself will set me free, from the hunter's snare.

From those who would trap me with lying words
— and from the hunter's snare.

Glory to the Father . . .
— God himself will . . .

CANTICLE OF ZECHARIAH

Ant. If your virtue does not surpass that of the scribes
      and Pharisees, you will never enter the kingdom
      of heaven.

INTERCESSIONS

Thanks be to Christ the Lord, who brought us life by his
    death on the cross. With our whole heart let us ask
    him:
    By your death raise us to life.
Teacher and Savior, you have shown us your fidelity and
    made us a new creation by your passion,
— keep us from falling again into sin.
Help us to deny ourselves today,
— and not deny those in need.
May we receive this day of penance as your gift,
— and give it back to you through works of mercy.
Master our rebellious hearts,
— and teach us generosity.

Our Father . . .

Prayer

Lord,
may our observance of Lent
help to renew us and prepare us

to celebrate the death and resurrection of Christ,
who lives and reigns with you and the Holy Spirit,
one God, for ever and ever.

Daytime Prayer

Midmorning

Ant. The time of penance has come, the time to atone
for our sins and to seek our salvation.

READING   Isaiah 55:3

Come to me heedfully,
  listen, that you may have life.
I will renew with you the everlasting covenant,
  the benefits assured to David.

Create a clean heart in me, O God.
— Renew in me a steadfast spirit.

Midday

Ant. As I live, says the Lord, I do not wish the sinner
to die but to turn back to me and live.

READING   See Jeremiah 3:12, 14a

Return, says the Lord,
  I will not remain angry with you;
For I am merciful,
  I will not continue my wrath forever.
Return, rebellious children, says the Lord.

Turn your face away from my sins.
— Blot out all my guilt.

Midafternoon

Ant. Armed with God's justice and power, let us prove
ourselves through patient endurance.

READING   James 1:27

Looking after orphans and widows in their distress
and keeping oneself unspotted by the world make for
pure worship without stain before our God and Father.

My sacrifice to God is a contrite spirit.
— A humble, contrite heart, O God, you will not spurn.

Prayer, as in Morning Prayer.

Evening Prayer

READING   James 5:16, 19-20

Declare your sins to one another, and pray for one another, that you may find healing. The fervent petition of
a holy man is powerful indeed. My brothers, the case
may arise among you of someone straying from the truth,
and of another bringing him back. Remember this: the
person who brings a sinner back from his way will save
his soul from death and cancel a multitude of sins.

RESPONSORY

To you, O Lord, I make my prayer for mercy.
— To you, O Lord, I make my prayer for mercy.

Heal my soul, for I have sinned against you.
— I make my prayer for mercy.

Glory to the Father . . .
— To you, O Lord . . .

CANTICLE OF MARY

Ant.   If you are bringing your gift to the altar, and
        there you remember that your brother has some-
        thing against you, leave your gift in front of the
        altar; go at once and make peace with your
        brother, and then come back and offer your gift.

INTERCESSIONS

The Lord Jesus sanctified his people with his blood. Let us cry out to him:
Lord, have mercy on your people.

Loving Redeemer, through your passion teach us self-denial, strengthen us against evil and adversity, and increase our hope,
— and so make us ready to celebrate your resurrection.

Grant that Christians, as your prophets, may make you known in every place,
— and bear witness to you with living faith and hope and love.

Give your strength to all in distress,
— and help us to raise them up through our loving concern.

Teach the faithful to see your passion in their sufferings,
— and show to others your power to save.

Author of life, remember those who have passed from this world,
— grant them the glory of your risen life.

Our Father . . .

Prayer

Lord,
may our observance of Lent
help to renew us and prepare us
to celebrate the death and resurrection of Christ,
who lives and reigns with you and the Holy Spirit,
one God, for ever and ever.

SATURDAY

Office of Readings

The man of God welcomes the light.
— So that all may see that his deeds are true.

FIRST READING

From the book of Exodus   12:37-49; 13:11-16

The Hebrews depart.
The law of the Passover and of the firstborn

The Israelites set out from Rameses for Succoth, about six hundred thousand men on foot, not counting the children. A crowd of mixed ancestry also went up with them, besides their livestock, very numerous flocks and herds. Since the dough they had brought out of Egypt was not leavened, they baked it into unleavened loaves. They had been rushed out of Egypt and had no opportunity even to prepare food for the journey.

The time the Israelites had stayed in Egypt was four hundred and thirty years. At the end of four hundred and thirty years, all the hosts of the Lord left the land of Egypt on this very date. This was a night of vigil for the Lord, as he led them out of the land of Egypt; so on this same night all the Israelites must keep a vigil for the Lord throughout their generations.

The Lord said to Moses and Aaron, "These are the regulations for the Passover. No foreigner may partake of it. However, any slave who has been bought for money may partake of it, provided you have first circumcised him. But no transient alien or hired servant may partake of it. It must be eaten in one and the same house; you may not take any of its flesh outside the house. You shall not break any of its bones. The whole community of

Israel must keep this feast. If any aliens living among you
wish to celebrate the Passover of the Lord, all the males
among them must first be circumcised, and then they
may join in its observance just like the natives. But no
man who is uncircumcised may partake of it. The law
shall be the same for the resident alien as for the native.

"When the Lord, your God, has brought you into the
land of the Canaanites, which he swore to you and your
fathers he would give you, you shall dedicate to the Lord
every son that opens the womb; and all the male first-
lings of your animals shall belong to the Lord. Every
first-born of an ass you shall redeem with a sheep. If you
do not redeem it, you shall break its neck. Every first-
born son you must redeem.

"If your son should ask you later on, 'What does this
mean?' you shall tell him, 'With a strong hand the Lord
brought us out of Egypt, that place of slavery. When
Pharaoh stubbornly refused to let us go, the Lord killed
every first-born in the land of Egypt, every first-born of
man and of beast. That is why I sacrifice to the Lord
everything of the male sex that opens the womb, and
why I redeem every first-born of my sons.' Let this,
then, be as a sign on your hand and as a pendant on
your forehead: with a strong hand the Lord brought us
out of Egypt."

RESPONSORY   See Luke 2:22, 23, 24

The parents of Jesus took him up to Jerusalem to present
    him to the Lord,
— because the law of the Lord prescribed
that every firstborn male had to be consecrated to him.

They offered to the Lord on his behalf
a pair of turtledoves or two young pigeons.
— Because the law . . .

SECOND READING

From the pastoral constitution on the Church in the modern world of the Second Vatican Council

(Gaudium et spes, Nn. 9-10)

Man's deeper questionings

The world of today reveals itself as at once powerful and weak, capable of achieving the best or the worst. There lies open before it the way to freedom or slavery, progress or regression, brotherhood or hatred. In addition, man is becoming aware that it is for himself to give the right direction to the forces that he has himself awakened, forces that can be his master or his servant. He therefore puts questions to himself.

The tensions disturbing the world of today are in fact related to a more fundamental tension rooted in the human heart. In man himself many elements are in conflict with each other. On one side, he has experience of his many limitations as a creature. On the other, he knows that there is no limit to his aspirations, and that he is called to a higher kind of life.

Many things compete for his attention, but he is always compelled to make a choice among them, and to renounce some. What is more, in his weakness and sinfulness he often does what he does not want to do, and fails to do what he would like to do. In consequence, he suffers from a conflict within himself, and this in turn gives rise to so many great tensions in society.

Very many people, infected as they are with a materialistic way of life, cannot see this dramatic state of affairs in all its clarity, or at least are prevented from giving thought to it because of the unhappiness that they themselves experience.

Many think that they can find peace in the different philosophies that are proposed.

Some look for complete and genuine liberation for man from man's efforts alone. They are convinced that the coming kingdom of man on earth will satisfy all the desires of his heart.

There are those who despair of finding any meaning in life: they commend the boldness of those who deny all significance to human existence in itself, and seek to impose a total meaning on it only from within themselves.

But in the face of the way in which the world is developing today there is an ever increasing number of people who are asking the most fundamental questions or are seeing them with a keener awareness: What is man? What is the meaning of pain, of evil, of death, which still persist in spite of such great progress? What is the use of those successes, achieved at such a cost? What can man contribute to society, what can he expect from society? What will come after this life on earth?

The Church believes that Christ died and rose for all, and can give man light and strength through his Spirit to fulfill his highest calling; his is the only name under heaven in which men can be saved.

So too the Church believes that the center and goal of all human history is found in her Lord and Master.

The Church also affirms that underlying all changes there are many things that do not change; they have their ultimate foundation in Christ, who is the same yesterday, today and for ever.

RESPONSORY   1 Cor. 15:55-56, 57; Lam. 3:25

Death, where is your victory? Death, where is your sting?

It is sin that gives death its sting.
— But thanks be to God,
who has given us the victory through our Lord Jesus
   Christ.

The Lord is good to those who trust him,
to all who search for him.
— But thanks be . . .

Prayer, as in Morning Prayer.

Morning Prayer

READING   Isaiah 1:16-18

  Wash yourselves clean!
Put away your misdeeds from before my eyes;
   cease doing evil; learn to do good.
Make justice your aim; redress the wronged,
   hear the orphan's plea, defend the widow.
Come now, let us set things right,
   says the Lord:
Though your sins be like scarlet,
   they may become white as snow;
Though they be crimson red,
   they may become white as wool.

RESPONSORY

God himself will set me free, from the hunter's snare.
— God himself will set me free, from the hunter's snare.

From those who would trap me with lying words and
— from the hunter's snare.

Glory to the Father . . .
— God himself will . . .

CANTICLE OF ZECHARIAH

Ant. If you want to be true children of your heavenly
      Father, then you must pray for those who perse-
      cute you and speak all kinds of evil against you,
      says the Lord.

INTERCESSIONS

To make us his new creation, Christ the Lord gave us
    the waters of rebirth and spread the table of his body
    and his word. Let us call upon him and say:
    Lord, renew us in your grace.
Jesus, meek and humble of heart, clothe us with com-
    passion, kindness and humility,
— make us want to be patient with everyone.
Teach us to be true neighbors to all in trouble and
    distress,
— and so imitate you, the Good Samaritan.
May the Blessed Virgin, your Mother, pray for all those
    vowed to a life of virginity,
— that they may deepen their dedication to you and to
    the Church.
Grant us the gift of your mercy,
— forgive our sins and remit their punishment.

Our Father . . .

                          Prayer
Eternal Father,
turn our hearts to you.
By seeking your kingdom
and loving one another,
may we become a people who worship you
in spirit and truth.

Grant this through our Lord Jesus Christ, your Son,
who lives and reigns with you and the Holy Spirit,
one God, for ever and ever.

Daytime Prayer

Midmorning

Ant. The time of penance has come, the time to atone
for our sins and to seek our salvation.

READING Revelation 3:19-20

Whoever is dear to me I reprove and chastise. Be
earnest about it, therefore. Repent! Here I stand, knock-
ing at the door. If anyone hears me calling and opens
the door, I will enter his house and have supper with
him, and he with me.

Create a clean heart in me, O God.
— Renew in me a steadfast spirit.

Midday

Ant. As I live, says the Lord, I do not wish the sinner
to die but to turn back to me and live.

READING Isaiah 44:21-22

Remember this,
   you who are my servant!
I formed you to be a servant to me;
   O Israel, by me you shall never be forgotten:
I have brushed away your offenses like a cloud,
   your sins like a mist;
   return to me, for I have redeemed you.

Turn your face away from my sins.
— Blot out all my guilt.

Midafternoon

Ant. Armed with God's justice and power, let us prove
ourselves through patient endurance.

READING   Galatians 6: 7b-8

No one makes a fool of God! A man will reap only what he sows. If he sows in the field of the flesh, he will reap a harvest of corruption; but if his seed-ground is the spirit, he will reap everlasting life.

My sacrifice to God is a contrite spirit.
— A humble, contrite heart, O God, you will not spurn.

Prayer, as in Morning Prayer.

Ant. 1 Jesus took Peter, Jam ̲ and his brother John
and led them up a high ̲ in. There he was
transfigured before them. ̲

Psalms and canticle from Sunday, Week ̲ 209.

Ant. 2 His face was radiant as the s ̲ and his clothing white as snow.

Ant. 3 Moses and Elijah were speaking him of the
death he would endure in Jerusa ̲ .

Reading   2 Corinthians 6:1-4a

We beg you not to receive the grace of God in vain.
For he says, "In an acceptable time I have heard you;
on a day of salvation I have helped you." Now is the
acceptable time! Now is the day of salvation! We avoid
giving anyone offense, so that our ministry may not be
blamed. On the contrary, in all that we do we strive to
present ourselves as ministers of God.

Responsory

Listen to us, O Lord, and have mercy, for we have
sinned against you.
—Listen to us, O Lord, and have mercy, for we have
sinned against you.

Christ Jesus, hear our humble petitions,
—for we have sinned against you.

Glory to the Father . . .
—Listen to us . . .

402-3-I

145

...ay of Lent

Sec...

CANTICLE OF MAR...

Ant. A voice sp...m the cloud: This is my beloved
Son in wh... well pleased; listen to him.

INTERCESSIONS

Let us give glo... God, who has concern for us all. Let
us call upo... and say:
— *people you have redeemed.*

Lord, save, ...and source of all truth, give the fullness

Giver of all ...ing to the college of bishops,
of your ...
— and ke... ll those entrusted to their care faithful to
the tea...ng of the apostles.

Pour yo... love into the hearts of all who share the one
brea... of life,
— tha... they may grow in unity in the body of your Son.

Help us to strip off our sinful selves,
— and to be clothed with Christ, your Son, the new
Adam.

Grant that all may do penance and find forgiveness,
— and so share in the fruits of Christ's redeeming death.

May those who have died in your peace give you everlasting glory in heaven,
— where we, too, hope to praise you for ever.

Our Father . . .

Prayer

God our Father,
help us to hear your Son.
Enlighten us with your word,
that we may find the way to your glory.

We ask this through our Lord Jesus Christ, your Son,
...o lives and reigns with you and the Holy Spirit,
... God, for ever and ever.

— Judah became God's . . .

SECOND READING

From a sermon by Saint Leo the Great, pope

(Sermo 51, 3-4. 8: PL 54, 310-311. 313)

*The law was given through Moses, grace and
truth came through Jesus Christ*

The Lord reveals his glory in the presence of chosen witnesses. His body is like that of the rest of mankind, but he makes it shine with such splendor that his face becomes like the sun in glory, and his garments as white as snow.

The great reason for this transfiguration was to remove the scandal of the cross from the hearts of his disciples, and to prevent the humiliation of his voluntary suffering from disturbing the faith of those who had witnessed the surpassing glory that lay concealed.

With no less forethought he was also providing a firm foundation for the hope of holy Church. The whole body of Christ was to understand the kind of transformation that it would receive as his gift. The members of that body were to look forward to a share in that glory which first blazed out in Christ their head.

The Lord had himself spoken of this when he foretold the splendor of his coming: *Then the just will shine like the sun in the kingdom of their Father.* Saint Paul the apostle bore witness to this same truth when he said: *I consider that the sufferings of the present time are not to be compared with the future glory that is to be revealed in us.* In another place he says: *You are dead, and your life is hidden with Christ in God. When Christ, your life, is revealed, then you also will be revealed with im in glory.*

This marvel of the transfiguration contains another lesson for the apostles, to strengthen them and lead them into the fullness of knowledge. Moses and Elijah, the law and the prophets, appeared with the Lord in conversation with him. This was in order to fulfill exactly, through the presence of these five men, the text which says: *Before two or three witnesses every word is ratified.* What word could be more firmly established, more securely based, than the word which is proclaimed by the trumpets of both old and new testaments, sounding in harmony, and by the utterances of ancient prophecy and the teaching of the Gospel, in full agreement with each other?

The writings of the two testaments support each other. The radiance of the transfiguration reveals clearly and unmistakably the one who had been promised by signs foretelling him under the veils of mystery. As Saint John says: *The law was given through Moses, grace and truth came through Jesus Christ.* In him the promise made through the shadows of prophecy stands revealed, along with the full meaning of the precepts of the law. He is the one who teaches the truth of prophecy through his presence, and makes obedience to the commandments possible through grace.

In the preaching of the holy Gospel all should receive a strengthening of their faith. No one should be ashamed of the cross of Christ, through which the world has been redeemed.

No one should fear to suffer for the sake of justice; no one should lose confidence in the reward that has been promised. The way to rest is through toil, the way to life is through death. Christ has taken on himself the whole weakness of our lowly human nature. If then we are steadfast in our faith in him and in our love for him, v win the victory that he has won, we receive what he has promised.

When it comes to obeying the commandments or enduring adversity, the words uttered by the Father should always echo in our ears: *This is my Son, the beloved, in whom I am well pleased; listen to him.*

Responsory   Hebrews 12:22, 24, 25; Psalm 95:8

You have come to Jesus, mediator of the new covenant.
Do not refuse to hear him.
— If those who refused to listen to him warning them
    on earth did not escape punishment,
much less shall we escape
if we will not listen to one who warns from heaven.

Today if you hear his voice,
harden not your hearts.
— If those who . . .

Prayer, as in Morning Prayer.

Morning Prayer

Hymn, 43.

Ant. 1   The right hand of the Lord has shown its
          power; the right hand of the Lord has raised
          me up.

Psalms and canticle from Sunday, Week II, 1220.

Ant. 2   Let us sing the hymn of the three young men
          which they sang in the fiery furnace, giving
          praise to God.

Ant. 3   Praise the Lord in his heavenly power.

READING   See Nehemiah 8:9, 10

Today is holy to the Lord your God. Do not be sad,
and do not weep; for today is holy to our Lord. Do not
be saddened this day, for rejoicing in the Lord must be
your strength!

RESPONSORY

Christ, Son of the living God, have mercy on us.
— Christ, Son of the living God, have mercy on us.

You were wounded for our offenses,
— have mercy on us.

Glory to the Father . . .
— Christ, Son of . . .

CANTICLE OF ZECHARIAH

Ant.   Our Lord Jesus Christ abolished death, and
       through the Gospel he revealed eternal life.

INTERCESSIONS

Let us give glory to God, whose kindness knows no
   limit. Through Jesus Christ, who lives for ever to in-
   tercede for us, let us pray:
   Kindle in our hearts the fire of your love.
God of mercy, let today be a day rich in good works,
— a day of generosity to all we meet.
From the waters of the flood you saved Noah through
   the ark,
— from the waters of baptism raise up to new life those
   under instruction.
May we live not by bread only,
— but by every word falling from your lips.
Help us to do away with all dissension,
— so that we may rejoice in your gifts of peace and lov